Introduction

If you love crafting, then chances are you have heard about the Cricut machine and all of the wonderful things that you can create with it. If you have heard of the Cricut machine, then you are more than likely thinking of buying one soon. Or, perhaps you obtained one and are now in need of a guide to find out everything about it.

I will help do a quick rundown about the Cricut with the goal that you can see all the wonderful ways to deal with utilize this workstation in your making needs.

Since Cricut started, there are presently a bunch of Cricut machines to choose from. So, which do you need?

All things considered, let me walk you through a differentiation data to give you a chance to find the ideal PC for your assignment needs.

<u>Machine comparison guide</u>

• Maker – Cricut Maker right away and unequivocally cuts more than 300 hundred materials, from the most unobtrusive paper and material to the troublesome stuff like matboard, calfskin, and basswood. Presently your inventive reachable is exponential.

• Explore Air – Performance meets esteem. Cricut Explore Air offers you the expert quality outcomes you need with the additional solace of Bluetooth network for wi-fi cuts and a twofold instrument holder for a messiness free condition.

• The Explore Air Two – Cricut Explore Air two is two times faster than all of the other models. It is able to cut a lot more as well as many other types of material, including iron-on, vinyl, and cardstock.

• Explore One – Cricut Explore One is an astute cutting figuring gadget for DIY activities and specialties that is anything but difficult to break down and simple to utilize. Cut, compose, and rating of 100 materials, for example, cardstock, vinyl, and iron-on.

<u>Cricut Maker</u>

The Cricut Maker is the most up to date propelled Cricut work area, and it has a ton of incredible highlights. They are fundamentally the same as the Explore line; however, they appear to lift a couple of more noteworthy advantages.

• Rotary Blade | They offer a rotating sharp edge that will diminish through material that is unbonded. That capacity you needn't bother with a stabilizer as the Explore machines require.

• Scoring Wheel | This is a pleasant improve from the Scoring Stylus. Spares time and introduces a smooth line.

• Knife Blade | You can utilize this to cut thicker calfskin and even articles like balsa wood, which is top-notch for making. two

• Basic Perforation Blade | Creates best tear-offs and easy strip aways utilizing paper, cardstock, acetic acid derivation, notice board, and that's only the tip of the iceberg

• Wavy Blade | Quickly make a charming wavy zone on a scope of well-known materials.

• Fine Debossing Tip | Customize activities with fresh, specific debossed structures – no envelopes crucial

• Engraving Tip | Engrave uncommon and everlasting structures on a scope of materials.

Cricut moreover presented here in July 2019; there will be a huge amount of new items pushed out available. When I get my hands on them, you can unwind guaranteed this will be your area to desire creates the use of the Cricut line!

<u>Explore Air and Air 2</u>

Both of these machines are a more prominent minimal effort alternative. Explore machines enable you to work with a scope of substances for your creating needs. Vinyl, cardstock, foils, sparkle paper, reinforced texture, and the sky is the limit from there. The biggest distinction between the Explore Air and Air 2 is the size contrast. The Air is a littler additional reduced measurement on the off chance that you don't format to do gigantic tasks, or conceivably have negligible creating space.

<u>Cricut Explore One</u>

Explore One is a work area that I propose to tenderfoots of making.

There are confined aspects anyway adequate that you can make and format exceptional specialties. This is the most reduced rate factor, too, so in the event that you are on a value go, this ought to be a perfect starter machine. At that point, as you study and develop, you can generally improve later to one of the different machines.

Any of the machines are great to claim, it depends on what you format to utilize it for, the zone you have, and what sort of specialties you sketch to utilize.

Which Cricut is best?

1. Cricut Maker | If you need every one of the fancy odds and ends close by with a brisk and calm machine.

2. Explore Air 2 | This is a more noteworthy reasonable processing gadget that comes shut to standing ensuing to the maker rendition!

Cricut has an absolute slew of items and materials. I adore Cricut Infusible Inks and Vinyl Projects; these are likely my top picks. What's more, they make planning easy with Cricut Design Space.

Possibly you got a Cricut work area for Christmas, or a birthday, however, it's as yet sitting in its container. Or on the other hand, maybe you're an eager crafter looking for a straightforward gadget to make making simpler. Or on the other hand, possibly you've considered huge amounts of cool endeavor photos on Pinterest and pondered, "How the hell do they decrease those muddled plans? I wanna do that!" Or maybe you've known about Cricut, yet you're asking, "What is a Cricut machine, and what would you be able to do with it?" Well, you're in the correct spot; today, I will acquaint you with the Cricut Explore Air machine and advise you pretty much all the cool things it can do!

There are no additional cartridges; the entire parcel is done carefully so you can utilize any textual style or structure that is on your PC. The Cricut machines are helpful to utilize, totally adaptable, and exclusively restricted with the guide of your own one of a kind inventiveness!

What is a Cricut Machine?

The Cricut Explore Air is a pass on cutting work area (otherwise known as specialty plotter or cutting machine). You can consider it like a printer; you take a photo or design on your PC and afterward send it to the machine. Then again, rather of printing your plan, the Cricut PC removes it of whatever texture you need! The Cricut Explore Air can cut paper, vinyl, texture, make froth, sticker paper, false cowhide, and that's only the tip of the iceberg! Truth be told, if you like to utilize a Cricut like a printer, it can do that as well! There is a highlight opening in the machine, and you can stack a marker in there, and after that, have the Cricut "draw" your plan for you. It's ideal for getting a top-notch written by hand appear to be if your penmanship isn't too extraordinary. The Explore gathering of Cricut machines favors you to get admission to a monstrous advanced library of "cartridges" rather than utilizing physical cartridges, as I did in school. This implies you can utilize Cricut Design Space (their on-line format programming) to take any content or shape from the library and send it to your Cricut to a. You can even transfer your own plans if you need!

The Cricut Explore Air can slice materials up to 12" enormous and has a little diminishing edge introduced inward the machine. At the point when you're prepared to lessen something out, you load the material onto a clingy tangle and burden the tangle into the machine. The tangle holds the fabric set up while the Cricut edge disregards the material and cuts it. At the point when it completes, you dump the tangle from the machine, strip your test off the clingy tangle, and you're outfitted to go!

With a Cricut machine, the odds are perpetual! All you need is a Cricut machine, Design Space, something to cut, and your own innovativeness!

Why it Has Become so Popular Today

The Cricut Maker is the most recent individual from the Cricut Cutting

Machine family! two This new workstation is incredible nowadays I'm sharing my Top 10 Reasons You'll adore the Cricut Maker, and it's more prominent than just the marvelous new Cricut ventures you might have the option to make! Truly I have in excess of 10 reasons, and I'll share them as well! From paper and vinyl to wooden and texture, there is no shortage of considerations and substances you can make!

You remember we cherish the Cricut Explore Air 2 for all its top-notch cutting and creating capacities. Well presently meet monstrous sister, and she's solid and inventive and prepared to make all the Cricut activities into the late evening! (Or on the other hand, till you come up short on coffee and head to sleep). The Cricut maker is the Cricut Explore with an all-out new arrangement of abilities. I believe you're going to love her! These Reasons Will Have You Cherishing Cricut. The Cricut Maker decreasing machine is fast, fantastic, and furnished to work with Texture! I was competent to see it live and face to face at an ongoing occasion facilitated by method for the Cricut group in Salt Lake City. The issues you have come to adore about the Cricut Explore family are all together in any case there. Presently there's even extra to cherish. I'm giving both of you records. They are really a similar rundown, anyway for these you that resemble me and pick a snappy answer at this moment, I have the best 11 brisk reasons. For completely every other person that needs the intricate details and the how's and whys, I'm clarifying more prominent about each component. How about we go!

The Best 11 Reasons Why You'll Fall in Love With Cricut

1.   Same reasonable yet better! – The same machine at the center with more highlights, power, and challenge conceivable outcomes

2.   Cuts material – New sharp edge, venture examples and tangle all planned particularly for developing with texture

3.   Sewing Examples from Effortlessness – 100's of sewing designs reachable in Configuration Space (with crease remittances)

4.   Turning Sharp edge – to cut material and a wide range of sensitive materials

5.   Blade Sharp edge – to decrease overwhelming duty materials like balsa and birchwood

6.   Versatile Apparatus Framework – to take into consideration additional diminishing control and more noteworthy gadget additional items later on

7.   More Stockpiling – the special Explore stockpiling is new and extended to give more noteworthy choices

8.   Print on Shaded paper – print on hued and designed paper with print-then-cut plans

9.   Gadget holder and charger – a region on the apex of the PC to hold your units and a charging port so you can cost while you make

10.   iOs and Android applications – the two iOs and Android clients can make in a hurry!

11.   Wonderful Plan Subtleties – same dazzling portrayal with brought little print and only a bit more prominent than the one of a kind Explore.

Top 11 Reasons – The Detailed List

If the short posting above sufficiently wasn't, here is my more prominent little print to see why you'll cherish these new components secured in the Cricut Maker. It's a dazzling PC with adequate flexibility and capacity to help make the undertakings you like to make. From paper artworks to little carpentry extends, this work area can make such a large number of particular plans and activities with you!

1.   The same magnificent PC is, however, shockingly better! – alright, this really is anything but another "reason" to cherish another machine. Aside from me, it is the additional fundamental reason I cherish this new machine. I, as of now, love my Cricut Explore Air 2. I cherish the use of Configuration Space, and I'm in all actuality satisfied with all the imaginative energizing I can have with this device. The Cricut Maker is only that, however far and away superior. There are more prominent highlights, additional abilities, moves up to things I as of now love and new things to attempt. Continue examining, and you'll understand.

2.   Cricut Maker cuts material – the new Cricut Maker has been re-engined to work with texture. It comes outfitted and arranged to make with another rotary cutting edge and explicit fabric one of a kind tangle. You study that right... texture! Presently, I perceive a few people have been cutting texture with their Cricut machines. I haven't had a lot of favorable luck with it. I've typically wanted to diminish fabric that I can use in my sewing venture, appliques, designs, and so on. Presently the Cricut Maker has been sketched to do just that! I tried the cutting abilities, and they are delightful. The same simply follows you'd foresee in the event that you cut by methods for the hand! Not a sewist? Forget about it! Crafters can join understanding that there is no texture we cannot create with the use of our Cricuts well, almost all materials. I haven't found one yet that I cannot cut.

3.   Sewing Examples from Effortlessness in Configuration Space

4.   Rotational Sharp edge –Not exclusively does this sharp edge cut texture pleasantly, it will likewise be you're a fine companion for cutting

refined materials. I hear it will decrease crepe paper splendidly! So, think. You're never again simply compelled to extravagant cardstock and specialty papers. We should test with every one of the substances from tissue paper to balsawood – the Cricut can adapt to it!

5.	Blade Sharp edge – Cut thicker substances with the new blade edge. Cut balsa wood or birchwood, or what about thicker cardboard or even chipboard. Presently your imagination can go even likewise with more noteworthy materials and cut alternatives!

6.	Versatile Device Framework – so you, as of now, analyze that the new Cricut Maker accompanies a rotating edge, and a blade cutting edge will rapidly be accessible. Things more decisions to come. This new Cricut machine has been intended to empower more prominent hardware as the group envisions additional gear to make. So, as they assume up additional approaches to enable you to make, the PC is set up for new hardware to be included… you'll simply need to sit back and watch what's straightaway!

7.	More Stockpiling – The pen holder on the Maker has been overhauled to protect extra of your instruments and embellishments. There is a profound cup and a shallow cup to get admission to a scope of things effectively. Also, the in-entryway complement holder has furthermore been overhauled to comprise of a couple of additional compartments. All your Cricut adornments have a home!

8.	Print on Shaded paper – What!? Truly, it is valid. The print-then-cut capacity is matched with the Cricut Maker to take into account imprinting on shaded and designed paper. You never again are limited to printing your Cricut structures on white paper. So proceed, get imaginative and print layers of workmanship and lessen your somewhat plans with extra breathtaking shading!

9.   Gadget holder and charger – We utilize our versatile units to make with our Cricut machines, and now the Maker has a district to put those gadgets while we chip away at our undertakings. Set your phone or work area in the device holder at the apex of the machine. What's more, there is a USB port on the Maker so you can connect your gadget and charge it while you are making. helpful, I state!

10.   iOs AND Android applications – You can set up your cut plans from anyplace with the cell applications helpful for the two iOs and Android. Effectively make the formats you want to make on your iPhone and keep for later at that point finish on your PC. You can ship plans to cut legitimate from the cell application or keep to your Structure Space account and get the right portion to it later.

11.   Delightful Plan Subtleties – really, the design is considerably prettier, and the measurement is marginally greater with the Cricut Maker. In any case, presently, not a horrendous parcel greater. The Cricut Maker will, by and by fit in your conveying case and should, in any case, fit on your favored art rack. They've also ensured some additional extravagant bling and finishing.

What Is A Cricut Machine?

The generic title for the Cricut is a die cutter, craft plotter, or a smart cutting machine. The format of this machine allows you to create projects from flat materials of varying thicknesses. The projects that you can do with this tool can range from simple to quite complex, depending on your skill level with these materials. Depending on the sharpness of the blade in your cutting machine, or the model that you're using, your materials can range anywhere from craft felt to thin sheets of metal. This gives you an idea of how vast the range really is, for what this machine can help you to accomplish as a crafter.

Other machines of this type can run you several hundred or even thousands of dollars, require design degrees, come with complex proprietary software, and offer only a fraction of the design options that come with Cricut, and the proprietary, user-friendly Cricut Design Space. Cricut's massive base of users are always sharing the latest and greatest in projects, tips, tricks, guides, and new materials to use with your Cricut machine. As a crafter with a Cricut machine, your resources are nearly limitless.

Thanks to the vast number of resources at our disposal as crafters, I've decided to compile the best of what's available, so you don't have to sift through anything confusing before getting started making your gorgeous projects and loving your new Cricut machine. In one organized place, you'll be able to access all the information you need on how to use the software, project guides that take you from start to finish, a list of all that you will need, and so much more. This is your comprehensive guide that you can refer to again and again, no matter how your skill level grows over time!

Just like with many other crafting media, if you're not paying attention, it is possible to spend more than you intended on materials, tools, accessories, and more. My intention is to show you which proprietary tools are worth the extra money, while showing you the best alternatives that you can use in place of other tools. Crafting is such a therapeutic and enjoyable experience; it shouldn't be prohibitive thanks to the cost! As you gain familiarity with the community of Cricut users, with the Cricut brand, I'm confident you will find the products and tricks that work the best for you in bringing your crafts to life!

Let's dive into how to choose the right Cricut model for you and for your needs!

How Can I Choose the Right Model for Me?

The wonderful thing about Cricut is that their models are all incredibly versatile and capable. Most capabilities that are had by one model will span the entire current Cricut line of products. There are some very minor differences in the ways in which they work and the complexity of their operation.

What's Available?

Thankfully, there is not a vast number of craft plotters available from Cricut at the time of writing, which means it will be really easy for you to take a look at all of what's offered without being overwhelmed. With huge product lines that contain many various models, finding what you want and need, while getting the most for your money can be a real chore. I'll outline each of the models currently available, what they can do, and what capabilities are best suited for what types of crafts.

Cricut Explore One

In terms of what is currently available from Cricut, this is the most basic machine they offer. This machine boasts being able to cut 100 of the most popular materials that are currently available to use with your Cricut machine, as well as being perfectly user friendly.

The Cricut Explore One is considered to be the no-frills beginner model of Cricut craft plotters and operates at a lower speed than the other models available. Unlike the others available in the current product line, the Cricut Explore One has only one accessory clamp inside, so cutting or scoring, and drawing cannot be done simultaneously. They can, however, be done in rapid succession, one right after the other.

While this is a great tool for a wide range of crafts on 100 different materials, and which can get you well on your way to designing breathtaking crafts that are always a cut above others, the cost is not as high as you might imagine. If you intend to use your craft plotter mainly for those special occasions where something handcrafted would be perfect, then this a great machine to have on hand.

At the time of writing this, the cost for the Cricut Explore One is $179.99

<u>Cricut Explore Air</u>

With all the capabilities of the Cricut Explore One and more, the Cricut Explore Air model comes equipped with Bluetooth capability, has a built-in storage cup to keep your tools in one place while you're working, so they won't roll away or get lost in the shuffle.

This model does have two on-board accessory clamps, which allow for simultaneous marking and cutting or scoring. These clamps are marked with an A and a B so you can be sure your tools are going in the right places, every time you load them in.

This model is equipped to handle the same 100 materials as the Cricut Explore One, and operates at the same speed, so the price difference reflects those differences and the similarities! This is a great value for the powerhouse that you're getting.

At the time of writing this, the cost for the Cricut Explore Air is $249.99

<u>Cricut Explore Air 2</u>

The Cricut Explore Air 2 is Cricut's current top selling craft plotter and is arguably the best value they have to offer for the price. This model cuts materials at twice the speed of the other two models, has Bluetooth capability, and has the two on-board accessory clamps.

The storage cup on the top of the machine features a secondary, more shallow cut to store your replacement blade housings when they're not in use, so that if you happen to be swapping between several different tips for a project, they're all readily available to you throughout your project. Both of the cups have a soft silicone bottom, so you won't have to worry about the blades on your machine becoming dull or scratched!

For someone who finds themselves using their Cricut with any regularity, this is the best machine for the job. You will be able to do your crafts twice as fast, and you will get a satisfactory result every time, even at that speed!

At the time of writing, the Cricut Explore Air 2 is priced exactly the same as the Cricut Explore One, at $249.99. If you're looking to jump on this, now is the time to get the best deal.

<u>Cricut Maker</u>

The Cricut Maker is considered to be Cricut's flagship model. This is the one that can do just about anything under the sun on just about any material you can fit into the mat guides of your machine. The one drawback of this powerhouse model is the price point. This does make this model more prohibitive, unless you plan to make crafts that you can sell with this model. If this is your intention, you can rest assured that whatever you turn out with this machine will be the best of the best, every single time. If you're selling your crafts, this baby will pay for itself in little to no time at all.

For the avid crafter who likes to show up to the party with the most gorgeous crafts that are leaps and bounds ahead of their peers, this machine might be overkill for the price. Of course, if you are keeping up with the Joneses, this is the model to have.

This model really does have it all and we can prove it. No other Cricut machine has the speed that the Cricut Maker has. The cuts that can be made with the special precision blades that fit only this machine, are crisper than anything you could ever hope for from a straight knife or other craft cutter. The blade housings allow you to simply remove the tip from the housing, install the next one, clip it back into place, and keep on rolling through your projects. In addition to this, the machine can detect the material loaded into it, so you won't need to set the type of materials at the beginning of each of your projects. With the other model, a common occurrence is that the project is halfway done before the crafter realizes that the dial is set incorrectly.

The machine, like some of the others, is fully Bluetooth capable, it operates with ten times as much power as any of the other models, it has a special rotary cutter attachment that allows it to glide effortlessly through fabrics and precision, and so much more.

At the time of writing, the Cricut Maker is priced at $399.99

Are There Older Models?

In a word, yes. There are several older models that have been phased out to make way for the Explore and Maker machines. The older machines were found to require a good deal more hacks, workarounds, troubleshooting, and understanding to get precise or even rounded cuts for the projects that crafters would like to do.

Here is a list of some of the models you may have seen in your travels:

- Personal Cricut Electronic Cutter Machine

- Cricut Create

- Expression 1

- Expression 2

- Imagine

- Cricut Mini

- Cricut Explore

Each of these models was compatible with a Cricut product called the Gypsy, which was not unlike the Cricut Design Space that we currently have today. Each of these machines had its triumphs in innovating the craft cutting processes.

The major aspect that Cricut aimed for overhauling when creating their newest line of models, was the complexity involved in working with their machinery. Communities of crafters had come together with hacks and math ledgers to program their machinery to work precisely as they wanted it to.

With the current line of available models, the Cricut Design Space allows you to be an innovative as you can possibly be with the design process, so none of your creative flow is eaten up by operations that should be taken care of by your machine.

If you own one of these machines, updating is certainly worth the money, but if it has served you well in your crafting, there is no need to upgrade. Cricut has always made quality products, and the cartridges containing various themed design elements are still supported through Cricut Design Space.

The Cricut Cartridge Adapter is a USB adapter, which allows you to import your cartridges into the Cricut Design Space, so all your elements are available in one organized space.

How To Use Cricut Machine

One of the greatest things about a Cricut is that it is extremely simple to use. It takes a while to get used to using it, but once you get the hang of it, only your creativity is the limit. Firstly, what comes with your Cricut? That depends on what product you purchase and the money you pay. The more you pay, the more you get.

These don't look like a lot of things, but they are all the right ones to get you started. For a beginner, it is recommended that you purchase a starter set which includes the necessary accessories.

<u>Setting Up the Machine</u>

The first step in the process of setting up a Cricut is to determine where the machine will be best located. Ideally, the machine will be placed near a computer or tablet, a power source and where it has room to work. Even if the machine does not require to be hooked to a computer, try to keep it within reach to make the process of loading and unloading easier.

The installation of a newer Cricut machine can be done in minimal steps. After the completion of all the installation steps you will start out with a free trial of Cricut Access, which gives access to additional projects, images. This trail cannot be paused so make sure you optimize the time of the trail.

To begin:

• Turn on the machine after it is connected to the power source.

• Use Bluetooth or the USB cable to connect the machine to the computer or your device.

• To set up a Cricut on a Mac or Window's computer;

• Go to the website for setup: https://design.cricut.com/setup

• If you do not have a Cricut.com account, create one to log in, or use your account information to log into Cricut.com

• When prompted, the Design Space plug-in should be downloaded and installed on the computer.

• Cricut Access will ask for acceptance of the terms of use to activate the free trial.

• When the prompt to make the first cut appears to set up is complete.

If you have any problems or the instructions are not clear; I highly advise you to visit the main Cricut website on how to setup your machine: http://help.cricut.com/help/manuals

Make Sure There's Space

The Cricut has to be set up with a space at the back of the machine as well as the front so that the mat can move freely as the blade cuts away. The risk of having your project fall to the floor if you do not have enough room in front and you are unloading is too big for comfort; that's why I prefer to be safe rather than be sorry. Keep that in mind when giving your Cricut its new home. There also needs to be space above your machine as you will have to open and close the lid to replace the blades, put in your markers and stylus, and work the buttons. Make sure that you do not stuff it in a tiny little shelf because that will end badly, I can assure you of that.

Opening and Checking

You can now open the box, breathe in, enjoy that new toy, and relish that butterfly feeling in your tummy whenever you take goodies out of the box. As with every new thing that you purchase, ensure that everything you ordered has arrived and that nothing is damaged. While this is a tedious step, no one wants broken items, especially since you are so excited to craft.

Placing and Taking the First Step

Once you have confirmed that everything is in an excellent condition, you can place your Cricut on its rightful area. The bottom will then drop slowly, leaving your machine open. Next, you can remove the foam packaging from inside the machine. You will notice that there are two clamps in the tool holder that had foam stuck to it. One is labeled "A," while the other one is labeled "B." Ensure that the blade is already in its clamp that is labeled "B," which stands for blade. "A" is for the accessories, e.g., your markers.

Following the Link

There will be a link on a piece of paper that you got with your box, which will take you through every step, ensuring that you setup your Cricut machine correctly. After following the guideline, you will then need to plug your power cable into both the Cricut and the power outlet. Congratulations - your Cricut is now alive!

Connecting to Your Computer

Now, you can turn on your machine.To connect the unit that requires the cable to your laptop, you simply have to put the square end in its designated place at the back of your Cricut and attach the rectangular end to the USB port on your desktop or Laptop.

If you have a wireless device, enable your Bluetooth on whichever device you wish to connect your Cricut to, open the Bluetooth settings, and pair with the machine. You will instantly recognize the name of your machine.

Now, you're all set!

<u>Cricut Software</u>

- Design Space

Design Space is for any Explore machine with a high-speed, broadband Internet connection that is connected to a computer or an iOS device. This more advanced software allows full creative control for users with Cricut machines.

- Craft Room

Some machines, such as the Explore and Explore Air, cannot use Craft Room, but many other models can. Craft Room users also have access to a free digital cartridge, which offers images that all Cricut machines can cut.

<u>Moving on to Creating Your Project Template</u>

On the home page, select "New Project", which will be followed by a page with a blank canvas that looks like the grid on your Cricut mats. To any artist, the words "empty canvas" is a nightmare in itself so please just bear with me since we will fill that bad boy up in a second. But first, let's go through the menu options.

New, Templates, Projects, Images, Text, Shapes, and Upload. These are the things that you will see on your left-hand side when you have the canvas open on the screen.

<u>Cricut Basic</u>

This is a program or software designed to help the new user get an easy start on designing new crafts and DIY projects. This system will help you with image selection to cutting with the least amount of time spent in the design stages. You can locate your image, pre-set projector font, and immediately print, cut, score, and align with tools that are found within the program. You can use this program on the iOS 7.1.2 or later systems as well as iPad and several of the iPhones from the Mini to the 5th generation iPod touch. Since it is also a cloud-based service, you are able to start in one device and finish from another.

<u>Sure Cuts a Lot</u>

This is another third-party software that has a funny name which gives you the ability to take control of your designs without some of the limitations that can happen when using cartridges used within the Cricut DesignStudio. You will need to install an update to your software to use this program; you can download it for free. It allows for the use of TrueType and OpenType font formats as well as simple drawing and editing tools. You can import any file format and then convert to the one that you need. There is an option for blackout and shadow.

<u>Cricut DesignStudio</u>

This program allows you to connect with your software and provides you with much more functionality as far as shapes and fonts are concerned. There are various options for tools that provide you resources for designing more creative images. You will be able to flip, rotate, weld, or slant the images and fonts. However, you will still be limited in the amounts or types of fonts that you can use based on the ones on the cartridges. There is a higher level of software features that allow for customization.

<u>Cricut Sync</u>

This is a program designed for updating the Cricut Expression 2 as well as the Imagine machine and the Gypsy device. You just connect your system to the computer and run the synced program for an installation of updates on the features that come with your machine. This is also used to troubleshoot many issues that could arise from the hardware.

Play Around and Practice

You can combine your shapes and images, add some text, and create patterns. The possibilities are endless. The best thing to do is familiarize yourself with the software before you attempt on cutting expensive materials. Start small and cheap - printer paper will be an ideal choice - and cut away. See what works well for you and stick with it. There are many options concerning the Cricut Design Space, and the only way to learn all of this is to experiment and click on every tab you see and try different combinations of options when playing around on the software.

Make the Cut

This is a third-party program that works with the Cricut design software. It offers a straightforward look at the design features that Cricut has. This system can convert a raster image into a vector so that you can cut it. There is also a great way to do lattice tools. It uses many file formats and TrueType fonts. There are advanced tools for editing and an interface that is easy to learn and use. This system works with Craft ROBO, Gazelle, Silhouette, Wishblade, and others. It allows you to import any file from a TTF, OTF, PDF, GSD, and so on and convert them to JPG, SVG, PDF, and so on. It is flexible and user-friendly.

Dials, Blades, and Settings

The speed, size, and pressure dials are the dials used to customize settings to various materials. For instance, if the material is thinner less pressure is needed from the blade than with a thicker material. On many machines, there is a Smart Set Dial. This is a setting that eliminates the need to customize speed, size, and pressure for each different material. Whether you are cutting card stock, vinyl, or fabric, etc. the Smart Set Dial setting will put the blade in the correct position for cutting. It is a great idea to buy many blades of various depth cuts. Thicker materials like leather, thicker card, and more require a deep cut blade which can be found at the Cricut shop at cricut.com. Currently, there are five available blades. The first is the fine point blade; this blade is used primarily for light to medium materials like paper, card stock, and vinyl. The fine point blade is a gold color. The fine point blade comes with the Cricut Explore One, Cricut Explore Air, and Cricut Explore Air 2. The next blade is the deep point blade, which is used for thick materials such as chipboard, foam sheets, and very thick card stock, etc. Thirdly, the Bonded Fabric Blade is used to optimally cut fabric that is bonded with the backing material. Next is the Rotary Blade. The Rotary Blade is not sold individually but it does come with the Cricut Maker and can cut any type of fabric. The Rotary Blade can cut fabric that is not bonded with backing paper, unlike the Bonded Fabric Blade. Like the Rotary Blade, the final blade is exclusive to the Cricut Maker and cuts stronger woods like basswood but is sold separately from the Maker. Whichever blade you choose to use make sure that the blade is Cricut brand. Using a non-Cricut brand blade can cause the machine to not cut properly. On many different blogs, there will be an example chart that shows which settings to use with each material. Even when using the settings from the chart try to do test cuts before the final cut to make sure that the settings are correct. Just like you would use cheap material like printer paper to do your first cut with your machine you should also use cheap material to do test cuts just in case something goes wrong.

The Cricut Cutter machine comes with a Standard Grip Cutting mat, but some materials require a lighter or stronger grip. To the right is a guide to show which strength mat you need to use for each material. Also, be sure to place the material or paper where the "Align Paper Corner Here" icon is. Placing the paper anywhere else on the cutting mat will either prevent cutting or cause a malfunction in the cutting process. The Cricut Cutter machine should load the mat and the material at that time if it does not select the Unload Paper button on the keypad and retry the process. When cutting materials do not attempt to cut on material smaller than three inches by three inches on all models except the Cricut Mini. The recommended size for cutting is six inches by twelve inches, especially for your first try cutting with the Cricut Cutter machine. It is also recommended to practice on cheap materials when first cutting to get the hang of using your Cricut Cutter machine. Although it can be expensive, it is suggested to keep many different materials on hand of various prices and thickness so that when you want to execute a project you already have the materials on hand. In addition, the Cricut Cutter machine comes with a Sample Project. Many Cricut masters and bloggers suggest that this be your first project. Trying to do a complicated project the first go around is not an intelligent or safe decision. Once you are done cutting select the Unload Paper key and take out the cutting mat. From there, slowly peel off the material or paper to avoid rips and damage to your creation; then peel away all excess material from the cut-out. The first time using the cutting mat can be difficult because the brand-new mat can be extremely sticky. It is a good tip to de-tack your cutting mat by placing a t-shirt on the sticky mat to get rid of a bit of the stick ness of the mat. Not doing this step increases the probability of destroying your creation when peeling it off of the cutting mat. Another quick tip is when removing access material from a very small design or intricate design use a lint roller. Roll the lint roller over the top of the design cutout to remove every little piece of material. When removing the cut out from the cutting mat use a scraping tool. Basic tools do not come with your Cricut Cutter machine, but they are quite useful tools and it is recommended to invest in the tools which can be bought at cricut.com. (Tools to use include the Cricut Blade, Hook, Scoop, and Scraping tools). Make sure to always remove all paper and or material from the cutting mat after each creation is made. Doing these steps ensures that the cutting mat will be fantastic at performing later. Also, it is recommended to keep the plastic covering that the cutting mat comes with. Put the plastic covering back onto the mat when finished cutting to keep the mat clean.

To recap, put the paper onto the cutting mat; then select load paper. Once the mat is inside select the cut button then presses unload paper when the cut is finished.

<u>Selecting Shapes, Letters, and Phrases</u>

However, in order for the cut to be made the machine must know what to cut. To tell your Cricut Cutter machine what to cut select the shapes, letters, and/or phrases you would like to cut out up to sixteen items. Whatever items you select should appear on your LCD display screen. Now that you know a few basic operations it is best to learn the functions of a few of the keys and buttons located on the keypad at the top of the machine.

<u>Keys and Buttons on Keypad</u>

Do not hold the shift button; it is only necessary to select the button then select the key with the shape or letter on the upper right corner that you would like. That shape or letter should then appear on the LCD display screen. When the shift key is activated it will be lit up.

The Shift lock key does the exact same thing as the Shift key except the Shift lock key allows for the repeated selection of upper right corner shapes and letters without having to keep selecting the shift key. Space and backspace keys work the exact same as space and backspace keys on a keyboard on a computer or other digital device. The space key puts a blank space between the two letters, shapes, or words. The backspace key deletes the last letter, shape or word selected from the LCD display screen. Most Cricut users do not use the space key as they cut one word at a time. It is recommended to use the space key when negative space in the cut is desired.

The Clear Display key, unlike the backspace key, will delete all selected shapes, letters, and phrases from the LCD Display screen. The Reset All key erases all settings on your Display screen returning all the settings to the factory default.

Create An Account On "Cricut.Com" And "Cricut Access"

"Cricut" is poised to become a one stop shop for all your crafting and DIY project ideas. Their "Design Space" application is developed to let the artist inside you flourish into the world of technological advancements. It is a free and easy-to-learn design software that can work with all kinds of "Cricut" devices. It is also a cloud-based application, which allows you to seamlessly access all your design files from any device whenever you need it.

The software is synchronized across your devices so you can start a project on your mobile phone when the inspiration strikes and pick it right up from your laptop. It also supports the integrated camera on your devices so you can view your designs on real-life backgrounds. You can then wirelessly connect the "Design Space" with your "Cricut Explore" or "Cricut Maker" to easily print and cut your designs.

Here are some of the amazing features offered by "Cricut Design Space":

- Seamlessly design and cut all your crafts with any of the "Cricut Explore" and "Cricut Maker" machines.

- Wide variety of selection from over 50k pictures, fonts and projects through the "Cricut Image Library". And you can also upload your own pictures and fonts absolutely free of any charge to create personalized designs.

- You will also be able to edit and enhance your uploaded pictures to take your projects to the next level.

- This application allows you to download pictures and fonts on your devices so you can continue designing and cutting your project even with no Internet.

- The "Make It Now" projects are carefully crafts so you easily design your ideas and quickly cut the any of the pre-designs, when you are running short on time.

- You can create decorations for holiday and party, cards, wedding invitations, scrapbooks, fashionable accessories and jewelry, personalized crafts for babies and kids, and the list goes on and on.

- By connection with "Cricut" machines, you can easily cut a range of different materials such as "paper, vinyl, iron-on, cardstock, poster board, fabric and even thicker materials like leather".

- You can create an account on "Cricut" for free and sign in with your "Cricut ID" to work on your fonts, pictures and projects. It would even let's you easily pay for any purchase made on "Cricut.com" or directly within "Design Space".

- The "Cricut" machines and "Design Space" support Bluetooth connectivity so your can wirelessly connect the software with your machines. However, some machine may require "wireless Bluetooth adapter" that you can easily purchase online.

Creating an account on "Cricut.com"

Now that you understand what "Design Space" is and how you can use to create beautiful DIY projects. Let's look at how you can get your own "Cricut ID" to log into the "Design Space" application.

1. On the official "Cricut" site, select *"Design"* from the top right corner of the screen.

2. A new window will open, from the bottom of the screen select   *"Create*

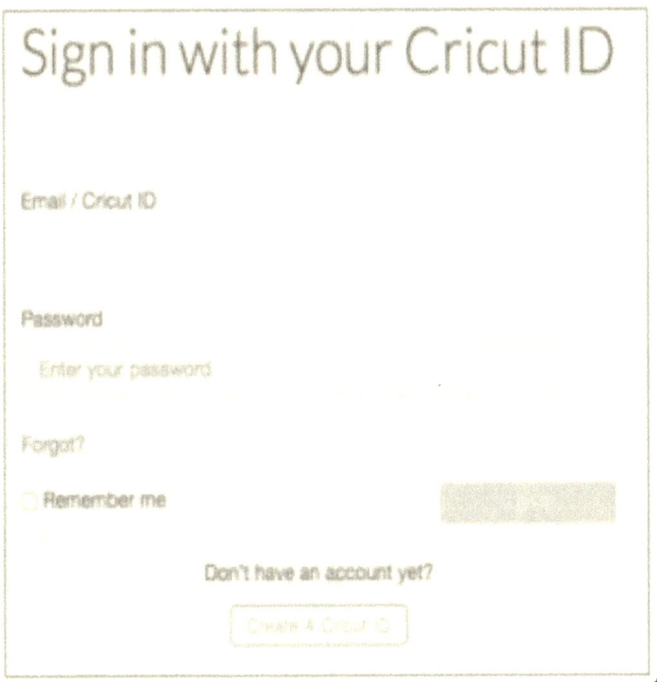

A

Cricut ID".

3. *Now, in the window as shown in the picture below, you would need to enter your personal information, such as, first name, last name,*

email ID and password.

4. You would then need to check the box next to *"I accept the Cricut Terms of Use"* and click on *"Create*

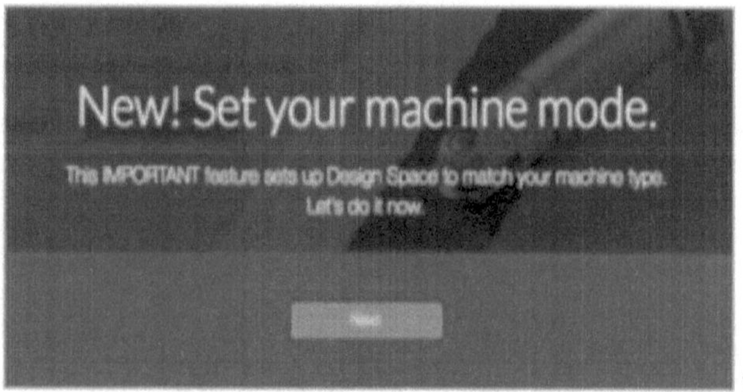

a

Cricut ID".

5. You will be instantly taken to the "Design Space" landing page and a message reading *"New! Set your machine mode"* will be displayed.

With the steps above you have registered your email address as your new "Cricut ID"!!!!

Now, let's see how you can complete your registration and start using "Design Space".

1. When you log into "Design Space" for the first time, your screen will display the message as shown in

the

picture below.

2. Click on *"Next"* as displayed in the picture above, a blacked out screen with *"Machine"* on the top right corner of the screen will be displayed as shown in the picture

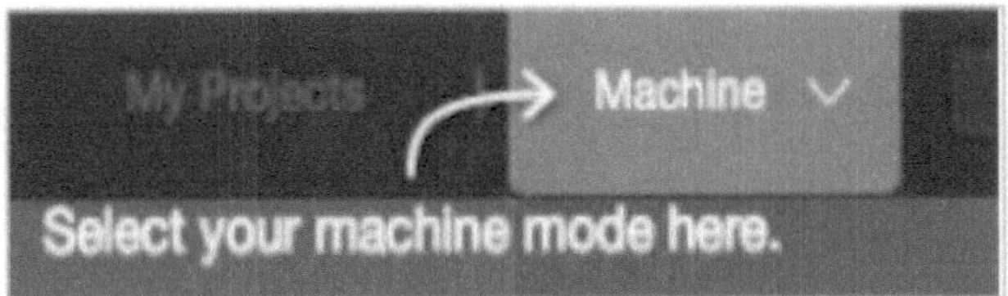

below.

3. Click on *"Machine"* and the options of the "Cricut" machines will be

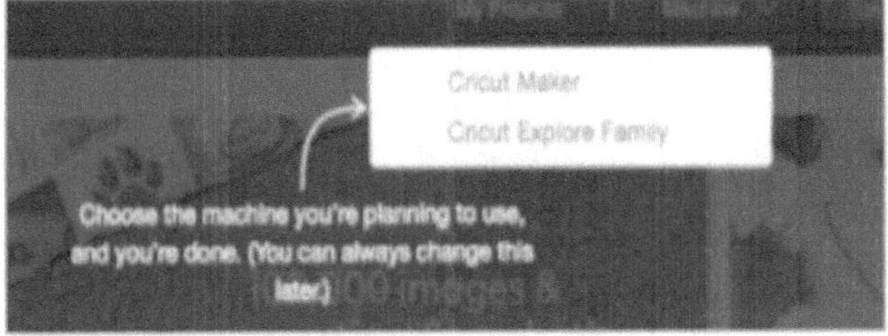

displayed as shown below.

4. You can select your device from the two options. For this example, "Cricut Maker" was selected and upon selection, the next screen will confirm the device you selected, as

shown in the picture below.

Remember, if you wish to toggle to the "Cricut Explore", all you have to do is click on the "Maker" and you will see the drop down option for the two machines again, as shown 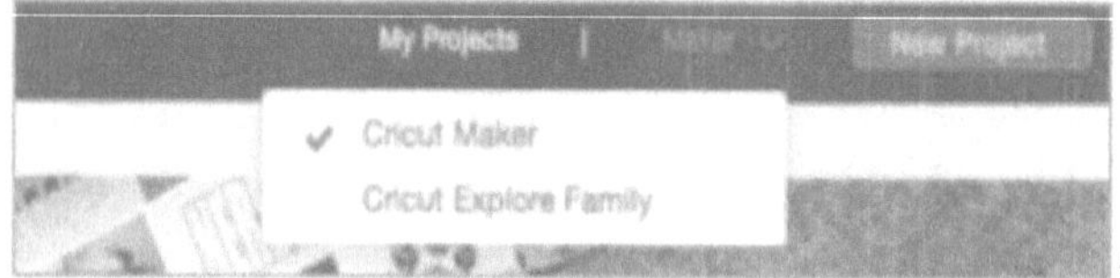 in the picture below.

Design Space on Mobile Devices

As mentioned earlier, the "Cricut Design Space" is cloud based and you can pick up your project across various platforms. Here's how you can download the latest version (v 3.18.1) of this application on your mobile devices.

Apple App Store (iOS) – Simply search for "Cricut" on the App store from your iPhone or iPad and select "GET" to begin the download. You can then easily login with your registered "Cricut ID" to continue working on your projects on your phone.

Google Play (Android) – You can search for "Cricut" on the Google Play from your android phone and table. Then select "Install" to begin the download. Once completed use your "Cricut ID" to login and pick up your projects and ideas where you left off.

Accessories And Tools

When you have a Cricut machine, there are a few tools that you would need which would make your crafting project easier and manageable. All these different tools help with cutting materials. The tools that you would need are:

Cricut Cutting Mat

For every Cricut Machine you have, the must-have item every crafter need is a cutting mat. This cutting mat enables you to hold any material you use while the machine goes through cutting it. These mats come in different grip strength and varying sizes. You can differentiate it by the colors it comes in based on the grip, so you do not confuse them. Some projects would require you to use the StrongGrip mat, whereas some projects work better using a mat suitable based on the materials you are using, such as fabric.

The outcome of your project depends on the kind of mat you use so choosing the right mat is imperative. The different types of mats available are the LightGrip Mat, StandardGrip Mat, StrongGrip Mat, and the FabricGrip Mat.

Cricut Bright Pad

This Bright Pad includes a five-brightness setting adjustable LED light. It makes your crafting easier, and it aids in illuminating extremely fine lines for tracing. It is extremely useful when you are weeding so if you do find that weeding is a challenge, then the Cricut Bright Pad will solve this issue for you as it makes this process easier.

Cricut Pens

Cricut Pens come in different colors and a variety of sets that make DIY projects such as gift tags, cards, invitations, and banners so much more creative and beautiful. Crafters usually use these pens when they need to Write and Cut. You can get the Metallic pens, Candy Shop pens, the Classic set, Gold set, and even one called the Seaside set.

Lint Roller

Yes, you read that right, get yourself a lint roller. It is useful for removing any unwanted pet hairs, dust or excess materials from your mats. Animal hairs are big problems as they stick to the adhesive mats like there is no tomorrow, but a lint roller works great if you want to get rid of them.

Scoring Stylus

Add a scoring stylus to your cart as soon as possible if you are a paper crafter. The tool is excellent for making paper baskets and boxes. It gives the products the professional, store-bought finish and makes them so easy to fold as the stylus already creates the grooves for folding your paper projects.

EasyPress

Invest in an EasyPress. This is perfect if you are interested in printing T-shirts or customizing pillowcases. Basically, anything you want to have printed; you are going to need one of these bad boys to do it. There are lots of bundles available on the Cricut website, and they can range from $119.99 (only the EasyPress) to $389.99 for a large bundle with everything you need to get started on your printing journey and so much more. The prices change depending on the size of the EasyPress, as well as the size of the bundle you wish to take.

Complete Starter Kit

The Complete Starter Kit is great if you don't feel like purchasing tools individually or if you'd rather follow protocol and purchase exactly what you need. The kit comes with all the essential items; that's why it is a great purchase. However, if you're tight on cash, buying the bare necessities will be best. This includes the materials you may require starting crafting so you don't have to worry about any list of items that need to be bought.

<u>Cartridge</u>

Cartridges are designed to help with the keyboard overlay that is needed for designs. The DesignStudio that is downloadable on the computer will help with developing the design that you are looking for. Each cartridge is designed to have a booklet to help you with how to use it. Each cartridge will only work for that specific overlay; however, a company called Provo Craft designed a universal overlay cartridge that will help with this single use overlay issue. This allows the DIY crafter to only must learn one keyboard overlay instead of multiple, giving them a much better chance of being able to learn the Cricut machine easily. Each Cricut, whether a cake version or a paper version, has a specific set of parameters that will be set to use for cutting. This makes each one of the Cricut machines specific to their use and a unique tool to have.

Buy a cartridge or several. Please do invest in these. They are amazing, and they aren't that expensive if you look around for clearance sales or marked-down prices on Amazon. There are so many cartridges to choose from; it's like a never-ending pit of creativity. The selection ranges from themed cartridges to ones that only have fonts. It's great for any project, and it saves you the trouble of struggling with Design Space and creating your own designs. They also come in neat little boxes that are so easy to store and always looks uniform.

Sharpies

Sharpies - you will not be sorry that you have them. Yes, the Cricut pens are cool, but they are overpriced. Purchasing some extra Sharpies – or any form of pens that can be manipulated into fitting into the pen holder – will work perfectly. You will have a variety of colors and save a couple of bucks in the process.

Doors

The door on your Cricut Cutter machine protects the machine when not in use. On many Cricut Cutter machines in various models, there is a compartment on the inside of the door to place any needed tools for crafting. If the doors on your Cricut cutter machine are not staying shut, make sure that you have taken out or unloaded any accessories in the machine's accessory clamp which can cause the doors to remain open.

Spatula

For lifting cut peace of papers from the cutting mat spatula is used. Other related things like some stuffed card can be used. But, as spatula is not expensive and specially designed tool, so its use is recommended. It does not harm your cutting mat. Removing gross and sticky material from spatula is easy.

Adhesives

Glue, gums are adhesives, choose adhesive of your choice from any well-known brand. Sticky material like adhesives should not be ordinary, purpose of sticking two things together must be fulfilled through your selected adhesive. Different sizes of glue coffee cups are available. Select any jumbo pack or coffee cup or according to your requirement. The drying time of glue also matters, so go for some very good adhesive.

Tapes

Without tape completing task is almost impossible. Consideration Points for selecting tape are it should be chemical or acid free and it should be very sticky. Glue is alternate for tape, but sometime glue also does not work like tape.

Scissors

Keep a pair of sharp scissors with you. Enough sharp to cut cards, ribbons and papers. Must buy a cover for scissors. Place it above the reach of children and in a place where humidity does not affect it. Neat paper or card cutting really affect your decorative work.

Tweezers

Sometimes you need to deal with very tiny papers. Tweezers work efficiently in holding that small piece of papers which usually turns, curves and torn during use. Sometime additional use of glue sticks two papers which are difficult to get separate tweezers are perfect helper at that time. Keep it while doing crafting you will be needing it.

Trimmers

Blades and trimmers are essential thing it helps in cutting papers very neatly and in desired shape without putting additional effort to create neat effect.

Stock of paper and cards Card are comparatively thicker than paper. They are different things. Buying a stock makes you tension free, either you do test cuttings or throw it in making unusual shapes for trail. They should be enough for, until your whole tasks get complete.

Blades

The blades are designed to cut specific textiles when using the Cricut. Every single Cricut machine that you can buy comes with your own specific blade for that machine. You can purchase other blades that would be even more useful for specific textiles. Many of them come with a German fine point carbide blade. This is a useful blade for all projects. However, you may want to invest in a deep cut blade eventually. This one provides an effortless cutting of a much thicker textile such as leather and wood. There is an individual housing that will be used for this specific blade that is different from the one that comes with your machine, so keep that in mind. There is also an option or a fabric blade that is bonded. This is used to cut fabrics that are already stabilized with some sort of heat-pressed bonding. In the Cricut Maker, you will get a knife blade and a rotary as well. These do not work in other Cricut machines though.

<u>Keypad</u>

The keypad allows you to input phrases and words to tell the Cricut what to cut out using the font in the cartridge.

<u>Buttons</u>

For the most part, all buttons are self-explanatory the on button turns the machine on, the Cut button tells the machine to Cut once the design is already in place, and the Stop button tells the Cricut machine to stop cutting once the design has been fully cut. It is important to not try to Cut or press the Cut button without a cutting mat in place and without a design and cartridge ready to go. Select the STOP button if you've made a mistake during the cutting process, the blade will stop cutting and from there you can correct your mistake. The Off button turns the machine off.

<u>Roller Bar</u>

The roller bar piece of the Cricut Cutter machine has wheels called star wheels. Star wheels allow materials to not shift when cutting. However, when cutting thick materials like felt and foam the star wheels can leave marks and indents in the material. To avoid this marking from the star wheels moves the star wheels all the way to the right side of the rubber bar one by one. If the cartridge is in the way of this maneuver turn your Cricut Cutter Machine off by selecting the OFF button and gently move the cartridge over to either side. To make sure that the material still is not passed over by the star wheels make sure the material has at least one inch away from the right side of the rubber bar where the star wheels are now located.

<u>Display Screen</u>

The display screen on your Cricut Cutter machine shows the design in which the machine will be cutting. The design can be edited on the display screen. Settings for your Cricut machine are also accessible through the display screen, such as: calibrating the screen and resetting the machine. A few common problems with the Display Screen include the LCD being unresponsive, the screen stuck on the End User License Agreement, the display screen being pixelated, and the screen stuck on the Tap to Zoom message. If you have any of these issues turn your machine off, then perform a hard reset. It is important to take care of your Display Screen as it is a vital part of your Cricut Cutter machine.

<u>Do I need all these tools?</u>

While these tools are all great in helping you create a project, you will be glad to know that you do not need to have every single tool mentioned above to use a Cricut effectively. However, among the must-have items are the mat and the tools mentioned in the Essential Tool Set. These are extremely helpful to complete your projects especially the ones with tiny cuts. A good way to begin your Cricut crafting journey is to equip yourself with the basics, such as the mat, the Tweezer, and the Weeder to start off and then slowly add on other items.

<u>Where do I get these supplies?</u>

One of the best ways to score a good deal with Cricut supplies that are good quality and the right ones is directly from Cricut. By signing up for their emails, you will be informed of any sale or discounts that Cricut has all the time. You can also go online and look out for crafters' blogs and craft sites that use Cricut, and you'll find codes that you can use to get 10% discounts on your purchases. Not only that, you can get free shipping. You can also check out your local craft store to see if there are any items at the clearance unit. Do take note though that some codes offered by crafts stores may not be applicable on the Cricut online store.

Another good place to purchase discounted or cheap Cricut supplies is on Amazon and even eBay.

Start Using Your Cricut Machine

<u>How to Set Up Your Cricut Machine</u>

There are different platforms you can use to set up your Cricut machine including Windows/Mac and iOS/Android platforms. I will briefly explain the steps for setting up your Cricut machine using any of the platforms, depending on the one available to you:

<u>For Windows/Mac:</u>

1. Use the power outlet to plug your Cricut machine.

2. Power ON your Cricut machine

3. Use the USB cable to connect your computer and your Cricut machine. Alternatively, connect via Bluetooth

4. Go to your internet browser and open it

5. Navigate to design.Cricut.com/setup

6. Follow to instruction on your screen to create your Cricut ID or sign in if you already have one.

7. Download the Design Space plugin when you are requested to do so.

8. Install the Design Space to your computer. To download the Design Space plugin and install it is super simple. To know that your setup process is complete is when you are prompted to start your first project.

<u>For iOS/Android</u>

1. Use the power outlet to plug your Cricut machine.

2. Power ON your Cricut machine

3. Pair your Cricut machine with your iOS or Android device via Bluetooth

4. Download the Design Space plugin and install it.

5. Launch the downloaded app

6. Create a Cricut ID to sign in and if you have one already, use it to sign in

7. Select the menu and tap Machine Setup & App Overview

8. Tap New Machine Setup

9. Follow the prompts on your screen to finish the setup

10. Again, to know that your setup process is complete is when you are prompted to start your first project.

Note that your machine is registered automatically during the setup process of your Cricut machine. There is no cause for alarm if, for any reason, you did not complete the process when you first connect your computer to your Cricut machine. Go to step 5 and continue from there using the on-screen instructions.

How to design with Cricut machine

I know that you have lot of ideas stuck in your brain and looking for a way to express them. What you need to do is set up your Cricut Explore Air machine, set up the Design Space, and start expressing those ideas immediately.

Working with Fonts in the Design Space

One of the unique features of the Cricut Design Space is the ability to brand your project with distinct fonts and text. Most project with Cricut machines start with the Design Space and you know what? There is more to it than meet the eye. Let me start with fonts in the Design Space.

How to Add Text to Cricut Design Space

1. For users of Windows, navigate to the left-hand side of the Canvas and select the Text tool. For iOS or Android user, the Text tool is at the bottom-left of the screen.

2. Select the font size and the font type you wish to use and then type your text in the text box. Do not freak out when you did not choose the font parameters before typing the text, with Cricut Design Space, you can type the text before selecting the font on Windows/Mac computer.

3. Click or tap on any space outside the text box to close it.

How to Edit Text in Cricut Design Space

To edit the text is super simple. Double click on the text to show available options. Select the action you wish from the list of the options displayed including font style, type, size, letter and line spacing.

How to Edit Fonts

1. Select the text you wish to edit on the Canvas or you can insert text from design panel, or select a text layer from the Layers Panel.

2. When the Text Edit Bar pops up, you can start changing the font using the available options. These options include Font, Font Drop-Down, Font Filter, Style, Font Size, Line Space, Alignment, and more.

How to Write Using Fonts

A simple way to write font using Cricut pen with Cricut Explore Air machine is to change the line type of your text from 'Cut' to 'Write'. Next is to choose the font type you wish to use and select the "Writing style" of your choice.

Note that the fonts used in the Writing style is similar to the text written by hand but the Cricut machine will write it as if it is tracing the outside of the letters. I believe you know how to use fonts now and what the final form of the fonts will look like. Now, I want to discuss the different types of fonts.

<u>System Fonts</u>

System fonts refer to fonts installed on your computer or mobile device. Every time you sign in, the Cricut Design Space will automatically access your system fonts and allow you to use them for free in the Design Space projects.

Some system fonts have design components that are not compatible with Cricut Design space because they were not designed by Cricut. Do not be surprise when you encounter failure to import them into the Design Space, or they behave unusual while using them in the Design Space. Use the instructions on the font site or app when downloading fonts to your device or computer.

<u>How to Use Images in Cricut Design Space</u>

The Cricut library has more than 50,000 images and these images are updated from time to time. The Cricut Design space permits you to use some of these images for free in order to find out if these images fit into your desired project before buying them. You can also upload your personally designed image unto the canvas. Here are simple steps on how to use image(s) in your project:

1. Sign in to your Design Space and create a new project

2. Tap on Image button in the bottom left corner of your screen if you are using iOS/Android device or click on Images at the left-hand side of your screen if you are using Windows/Mac computer.

3. Browse the images to choose the ones you wish to use in your project. Use any of the options below:

- All Images—use this to search for a particular image in your Library or view featured images.
- Categories—use this to browse images by selecting the image categories.
- Cartridges—use this to search through the alphabetical list of more than 400 Cricut cartridges or even search for a specific one.

4. Insert your desired image(s) into your project and start editing them.

<u>How to Cut One Image out of Another Image</u>

It is possible to remove a part of an image to form another image using the Slice tool in Design Space and is super easy too. Use these steps to remove an image out of another image:

1. Position the two images to overlap each other.

2. Select the two images.

3. Click on "Slice". This button is at the bottom of the Layers Panel for computer users, in the Actions' menu at the bottom of the screen for Android and iOS users.

4. Separate the layers to check your new shapes.

5. Edit or delete the images separately.

6. Go to Layer and slice your image till you get your desired design.

<u>How to Upload Images on Cricut Design Space</u>

There are two types of images that you can upload to the Design Space which are Basic and Vector images. Basic images include file type like .jpg, .gif, .bmp, and .png while Vector images include files such as .svg and .dxf.

Here are the step by step instructions on how to upload images on Design Space via different platforms:

On Windows/Mac

1. Select Upload on the design panel on the left-hand side of the Canvas.

2. Use the Browse button to find your desired image from the computer or drag and drop the file to the upload window.

3. To upload Basic images, use these steps:

- Select your desired basic image file, select Open or drag and drop the file unto the Design Space
- Describe your image on the screen as either simple, moderately complex or complex
- Select Continue
- Define the cut lines of your image by editing unwanted background.
- Select the Preview to view the cut lines of your image. If you are satisfied with the image, select Continue.
- Name your image and tag it. Also decide how you intend to save it, either as Cut or Print and Cut image. Note that saving your image as Print Then Cut will save the entire image.
- Select Save when you are done.

4. If on the other hand, you intend to upload Vector image, then use these

steps:

- Select the Vector image file you wish to upload then select Open or use drag and drop the file unto the Design Space.
- Name your image and tag it as stated in Basic image option.
- Click the image and select insert images to include it on your design screen.

<u>On iOS device:</u>

1. Tap the Upload tool at the bottom toolbar.

2. Choose Browse files to search the image you intend to upload from the available storage applications on your device.

3. If it is Basic image, clean the image and define the cut lines of the image. You can use these options:

- Remove-this will remove connected areas having the same color.
- Erase- Use this option to remove unwanted areas of the image you wish to eliminate.
- Crop- use this option to trim the edges of your image.

4. After cleaning your image, select Next at the upper right corner of your screen

5. Make final adjustments at your image before you save it your library.

6. Tap Next

7. Name your final image and save it either as Cut image or Print Then Save.

8. Click Save at the upper right corner of your screen.

9. Select the image to insert unto the Canvas from the Uploaded images

library.

1. Tap the Upload button at the bottom panel

2. Choose to take a photo, choose from the photo library or open uploaded images

3. Select the file storage application where your image is located

4. For Vector images, enter the name and tap "Save".

5. For Basic images, use the options Remove, Erase and Crop to modify your image.

6. Click Done when you have finished cleaning the image.

7. Tap Next at the upper right corner of the screen.

8. Name your image and choose how to save it.

9. Select the image you wish to upload unto the Canvas.

Making Your First Project Ideas

Now that you have all of your goodies, what happens next? You might feel a little overwhelmed by the endless possibilities and wonder what you can do afterward. I stared at my Cricut Maker for two whole days, contemplating whether I should dare to start a project or not. My mother, being the curious cat that she is, used my own machine before me because I didn't want to mess anything up. I had her set it up, learn how to work the unit, and then show me what to do. You might think it was silly, but to me, it wasn't. I neither want to become disappointed nor break or mess with any of the settings. It's not as if that is actually that easy to do, but I still had that fear. It was the most expensive thing I had bought for myself in a very long time so the moment was big. The fact that my mother was figuring it out before me pulled me out of that hole, and I realized that if she could do it - the squinting, index finger typer – then it was possible for me too. After that day, I learned everything else myself and discovered that it's really so simple. I still feel silly about being so scared about the instructions that happen to be as clear as day. I am grateful that I had someone to kick me into a start, although you don't need someone to show you how or force you to do that because all you have to do is follow the guidelines. All of your answers will be answered shortly.

In your box, you will find everything you need to do your first project. This is very cute to me. It does not matter if you didn't purchase additional tools or materials because the basics are there, and you can give the machine a go! It really is a very considerate thing to add to the box, and I am truly happy about that. Many people would have forgotten to buy supplies because they are so excited for their Cricut. And since it is your first practice project, if you mess up, you won't be ruining those pretty materials that you have already purchased.

After setting up your Cricut machine according to the instruction, there will be directions on your screen that you must follow to create your first project. You will still be using the link you found on the paper when you were setting up your machine. If you have not yet received your machine and are interested in knowing how it works, or you are looking for extra clarifications, here's what it will say.

First Step

First off, load a pen into the accessories clamp. You can pick whichever color you think will go best with the paper you have received. Next, you want to turn the knob so that the indicator is pointed to "cardstock", considering that is what you will be working with. Have you had a proper look at your mats yet? The blue mat is what you will want to use for this project. You should remove the plastic cover - keep it, don't throw it away as you will need to re-cover your mat when you're done to avoid dust accumulation - and lay down the paper on the mat with the top left corners of the material and the grid aligned.

Second Step

Make sure that the paper is pressed flat before you push it between the rollers firmly. The mat has to rest on the bottom roller. When it is in place, press the "Load" button to load your mat between the rollers. Press the "go" button, which will be flashing at this stage, and wait for the machine to work its magic on your project. It's really cool to watch this process unfold. Once everything is done, the light will flash, and you can press the "Load" button again to unload the mat. Your paper will still be sticking to the mat when you remove it.

Third Step

Be careful when removing the material from the mat. Don't be too hasty; take your time so that it doesn't tear. Pull the mat away from the cardstock instead of doing it the other way around. After completing that step, you can now fold the cardstock in half, insert the liners into the corner slots of the card, and it's done!

You're Done!

You have just made your first ever Cricut project in a matter of minutes from start to finish! Congratulations! What are you waiting for? Go make more projects! There are a ton of templates you can play around with. Practice, practice, practice.

Personalized Ideas, Accessories and Stickers

As you become more familiar with your Cricut machine you will become more creative, and you will soon find yourself coming up with new project ideas all day long. The Cricut website and Design Space are both great tools for project ideas to help get you started if you are not sure what type of project you would like to begin. Pinterest is also another great online resource for project ideas at different levels of difficulty.

Always keep in mind when starting a new project that you first must have all of the materials necessary to complete the project. It is always helpful to check your stock of tools and materials before getting started. The worst feeling is when you sit down and begin working on a difficult project only to realize you are out of a specific material needed to finish the job. It will save you a lot of time in the long run if you spend a few minutes at the beginning taking stock of your inventory! Working with materials you already have on hand is also a great way to keep your crafting costs low. It will always feel good to know that you made a custom piece of work without spending a ton of extra money just to complete it!

<u>Vinyl</u>

Creative Custom Vinyl Candles

Supplies Needed:

- Cricut Essential Tool Set

- Cutting Mat

- Transfer Tape

<u>Step One: Pick your Quote and Design it in Design Space</u>

Be sure to select a font that is easy to read. There are many different quote options already predesigned in Design space that you will have immediate access to. You will also have access to quite a few more design ideas for free if you are a Cricut Access Member. Here you can change the font size, color, and script. Once you have your design just as you want it, you can move on to the next step!

<u>Step Two: Measure, Cut and Place Vinyl on your Mat</u>

You will want to start this project by selecting the type of vinyl you want to use, in this project I would recommend permanent vinyl. You will then want to grab your 12"x12" mat with either standard or light grip. This type of mat usually works best with vinyl material. You will want to line up the vinyl to the grid on the cutting mat. This grid lines up with the grid in design space (if you choose to have the grid showing while you design). This will help you minimize waste as you can cut off only the exact amount of material you need to complete this project.

<u>Step Three: Cut Out Vinyl</u>

Before cutting, ensure that your Cricut machine is set to the right setting to cut vinyl. You can select a thin vinyl setting or set the cut to a thicker level, just to ensure that the Cricut machine cuts all the way through the vinyl on the first go round. You will want to back to stay intact, however (this will make weeding a lot easier when you get to this in the next stop) so don't overdo the cut pressure. Once you are secure in your vinyl placement on the mat, as well as your machine setting you are ready to go! Once the mat is loaded and the cut button on your Cricut Machine is blinking, you are ready to hit the button and begin cutting. Design Space will give you a percentage as to how far into the project it has cut.

Step Four: Remove Vinyl from Mat and Begin Weeding

This step is where you will need your trusty Cricut Weeder! You will want to remove all of the excess vinyl away from the cut that you want to put on your candle. Weeding can be tedious, and you will either end up loving it or hate it! This part of the project will also take some time depending on how difficult a design you choose. This is also a great step in a project to use your Cricut Bright pad if you have one. This will help illuminate the cut lines and help you differentiate between the excess vinyl and the pieces you want to keep. A wise investment if you truly enjoy intricate cut pieces with lots of weeding!

Step Five: Apply Transfer Tape

Transfer Tape is the material that will allow you to remove your vinyl design from its original backing and place it onto your project surface. The transfer tape will attach to the front of the vinyl, which is not sticky, and pull it from its original backing to expose the sticky side of the vinyl. You will want to ensure your design is fully stuck to the transfer tape before trying to remove it from the original backing. It is strongly recommended to smooth the transfer tape over your original design using your Cricut Scraper. This will also help you remove any air bubbles that may develop during the transfer tape applied to your design. Once you feel your design is securely stuck to the transfer tape, begin removing the design from the original backing.

Once your design is removed from the original backing you are ready to apply the design to your project surface via the transfer tape. You will want to follow the same process of smoothing the design onto the surface with your Cricut scraper and removing all of the air bubbles that will likely develop because the surface of a candle is typically curved. Transfer tape is usually fairly forgiving if you need to remove the design and reposition it before starting over. Once you feel your design is full stuck onto the project surface, you can begin to slowly remove the transfer tape. It should easily come off of the design, while the design continues to stick to the project surface. If you find that the transfer tape is pulling the design off of the project surface, stop and smooth the design back onto the project surface again with your scraper. You may have to do this a few times before the vinyl will stick. Once you have the vinyl fully stuck with the transfer tape removed, your project is complete!

You will follow a similar guideline for any type of vinyl project you may choose. There will always be adjustments depending on the type of vinyl you are using and the difficulty of the cut. Ultimately if you follow this step by step guide you will easily be creating multiple vinyl projects. Similar vinyl projects include coasters, drink cups, and car window monograms. This sample project is a great way to get started in the vinyl world.

Leather

Leather Pouch

Supplies Needed:

- Cricut Brand Genuine Leather

- X-actor knife or rotary cutter

- Deep Cut Blade

- Cricut Strong grip cutting mat

- Scoring Tool

- Heavy Duty Snaps

- Fabric Adhesive

<u>Step One: Set Up Your Machine and Leather on the strong grip cutting mat</u>

The first thing you will need to do is load up your machine with the genuine leather already pressed into a strong grip mat. This will ensure that the leather will not bump into the black bumper as it feeds into the machine. You will also want to cut down the right edge of the piece of genuine leather as it only needs to be 11 inches wide. Then you will want to move the four-star wheels or the little white wheels on your Cricut machine, over to the right so that you can run the material without bumping the wheels. Next and most importantly you will want to load your deep cut blade before starting this project.

<u>Step Two: Loading the design pattern into Design Space</u>

There is a premade design ready to go with Cricut Access in Design Space. The best thing about Cricut Access premade designs is that all you have to do is hit "make it" and it will load all of the materials settings, there is no need to size it! Select your machine and material. Note: If you are using the Cricut Explore make sure you have the dial turned to Custom in order to get all these options. This is where you will want to load your scoring tool to the accessories slot as well.

<u>Step Three: Hit "Go" and watch the Cricut machine to make magic!</u>

It is also recommended to go a test piece before running an entire sheet of leather into the machine. Similar to measure first cut once, always run a test design with scraps left over from prior projects!

<u>Step Four: Add Snaps and Glue in Flaps</u>

You will want to follow the directions on your snap kit to learn how to properly install the snaps on your leather pouch. You will want to glue the flaps in last so that you can ensure it lines up with the snaps secured.

The leather project above gives you a great opportunity to take advantage of the predesigned projects that are readily available with Cricut Access in Design Space. This one does require more technical advantages and has a higher degree of difficulty over the vinyl project also recommended. Safety always comes first, and it is recommended you read through the entire instructions to a project such as this before beginning the project yourself. It is also a good idea to have a helper on hand in the event you will need another pair of hands. Once you have a few practices rounds under your belt you should feel more comfortable doing this project on your own.

We sincerely hope you enjoy these sample projects we have provided for you. These are just two samples of what your new Cricut machine is capable of making. Anything you can dream up is an option for you to make on your Cricut machine, and this probably why the machine has gotten so popular in recent years! Feel free to begin your Cricut journey with these projects and others that are free for Cricut users all over the internet. Always remember that Cricut access is also a great resource for finding premade and designed projects ready to go!

Complex Operations

Cricut machines are pretty straightforward with what you need to do in order to make simple designs, but you might wonder about some of the more complex operations. Here, we'll tell you how to accomplish these with just a few simple button presses.

<u>Blade Navigation And Calibration</u>

The blades that come with a Cricut machine are important to understand, and you will need to calibrate your blades every single time you use your machine.

Each blade needs this because it will help you figure out which level of depth and pressure your cut needs to be. Typically, each blade needs to be calibrated only once, which is great, because then you don't have to spend time doing this each time. Once you've done it once, it will stay calibrated, but if you decide to change the housings of the blades or if you use them in another machine, you'll need to calibrate it again.

So, if you plan on using a knife blade and then a rotary blade, you'll want to make sure that you do recalibrate – and make sure you do this before you start with your project. It is actually incredibly easy to do this though, which is why it's encouraged.

To calibrate a blade, you just launch the Design Space, and from there, you open the menu and choose calibration. Then, choose the blade that you're going to put in. For the purpose of this explanation, let's say you're using a knife blade.

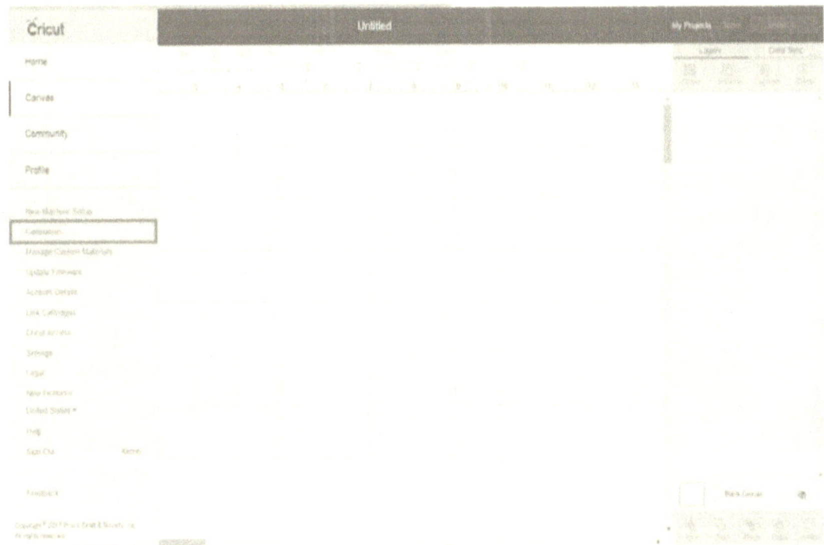

Put that blade in the clamp B area and do a test cut, such as with copy paper into the mat, and then load that into the machine.

Press continue, then press the go button on the machine. It will then do everything that you need for the item itself, and it will start to cut.

You can then choose which calibration is best for your blade, but usually, the first one is good enough.

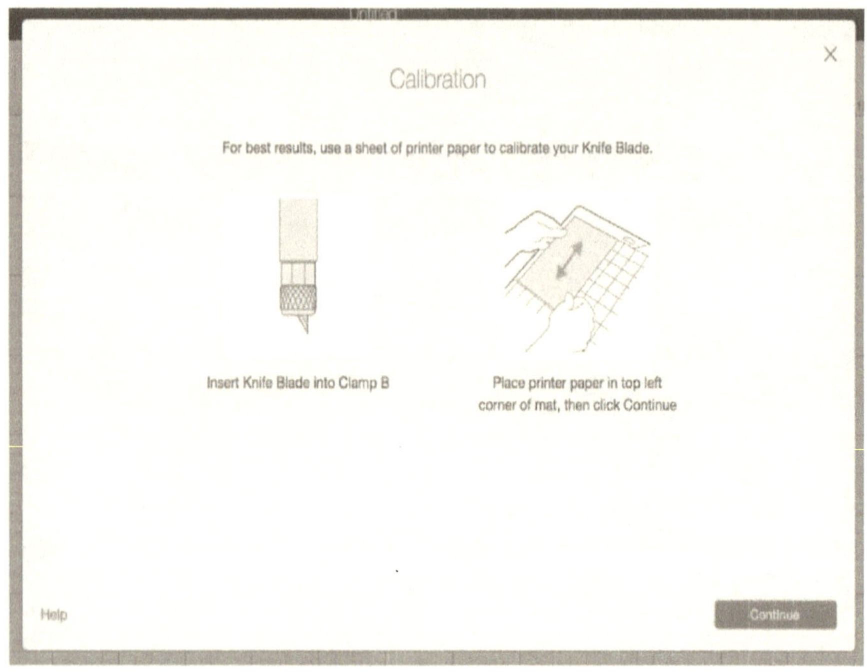

You can do this with every blade you use, and every time you use a new blade on your machine, I highly recommend you do this – for best results, of course.

<u>Set Paper Size</u>

Setting paper size in a Cricut machine is actually pretty simple. You will want to use this with either cartridge or with Design Space for what you'd like to make. This also comes with a cutting mat, and you'll want to load this up with paper so that you can use it.

To do this, you'll want to make sure that you have it plugged in, then go to the project preview screen. If you choose a material that's bigger than the mat size, it will automatically be changed, and it'll be adjusted as necessary based on the size of the material that you select.

You can choose the color, the size of the material, whether or not it'll mirror

– and you can also choose to fully skip the mat, too, if you don't want that image printed just yet.

Note that the material size menu does offer sizes that are bigger than the largest mat available.

If you're planning on using the print then cut mode, do understand that it's limited to a print area of 8.5x11 inches, but again, you can choose these settings for yourself.

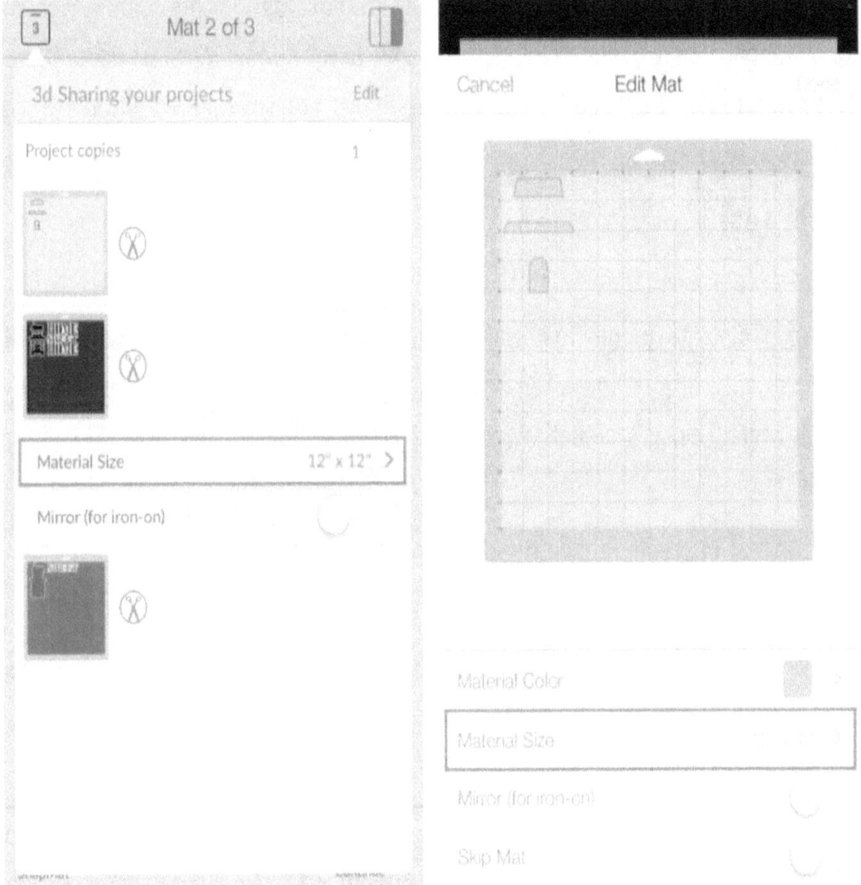

Load Last

To load that paper and image last is pretty simple. Remember that "skip this mat" step? Literally, press that, and then go. You'll be able to skip this quite easily. It's one of those operations that's definitely a little different from what you may be used to, but if you want to skip design and don't want to work with it just yet, this is probably the best option for you to use. If you're worried about forgetting it, don't worry – Cricut will remind you.

<u>Paper Saver</u>

Saving paper is something you'll want to consider doing with a Cricut machine because it loves to eat up the paper before you even start decorating. The Explore Air 2 definitely will appreciate it if you save paper, and there are a few ways to do so.

The first one is, of course, to halve your mats. But you don't need to do only that.

You can also go to the material saver option on the machine, which will automatically adjust and align your paper as best it can. Unfortunately, on newer machines, it's actually not directly stated, but there is a way to save paper on these.

You'll want to create tabbed dividers to organize your projects and save them directly there.

The first step is to create a background shape. Make sure that the paper looks like a background. Go to shapes, and then select the square to make the square shape.

Next, once you've created squares to represent the paper, arrange this to move to the back so that the shapes are organized to save the most space on each mat. Then organize the items that are on top of where the background is and arrange them so they all fit on a singular mat.

Rotating is your best friend – you can use this feature whenever you choose objects, so I do suggest getting familiarized with it.

Next, you hide the background at this point, and you do this by choosing the square, and in Design Space, literally hiding this on the right side. Look at the eyeball on the screen, and you'll see a line through the eyeball. That means it's hidden.

Check over everything and fine-tune it at this point. Make sure they're grouped around one object, and make sure everything has measurements. Move these around if they're outside of the measurements required.

Once they're confirmed, you then attach these together on the right-hand side of Design Space, which keeps everything neatly together – they're all cut from the same sheet.

From here, repeat this until everything is neatly attached. It will save your paper, but will it save you time? That's debatable, of course.

<u>Speed Dial</u>

So, the speed dial typically comes into play when you're setting the pressure and speed. Fast mode is one of the options available on the Explore Air 2 and the Maker machines, which make the machine run considerably faster than other models. You can use this with vinyl, cardstock, and iron-on materials. To set this, go to the cut screen. You'll have a lot of speed dials here, and various different settings. If you have the right material in place when choosing it, you'll be given the option to do it quickly with fast mode. From there, you simply tap or click on that switch in order to toggle this to the position for on. That will activate fast mode for that item.

It will make everything about two times faster, which means that if you're making complex swirl designs, it will take 30 seconds instead of the 73-

second average it usually takes.

However, one downside to this is that because it's so fast, it will sometimes make the cuts less precise – you'll want to move back to the regular mode for finer work.

This is all usually set with the smart-set dial, which will offer the right settings for you to get the best cuts that you can on any material you're using. Essentially, this dial eliminates you having to manually check the pressure on this.

To change the speed and pressure for a particular material that isn't already determined with the preset settings, you will need to select custom mode and choose what you want to create. Of course, the smart-set dial is better for the Cricut products and mats. If you notice that the blade is cutting too deep or not deep enough, there is a half-settings option on each material that you can adjust to achieve the ideal cut.

Usually, the way you do this with the pre-set settings is to upload and create a project, press go, and load the mat, then move the smart-set dial on the machine itself to any setting. Let's select custom and choose the speed for this one.

In Design Space, you then choose the material, add the custom speed, and you can adjust these settings. You can even adjust the number of times you want the cut to be changed with the smart-set dial, too. Speed is something you can adjust to suit the material, which can be helpful if you're struggling with putting together some good settings for your items.

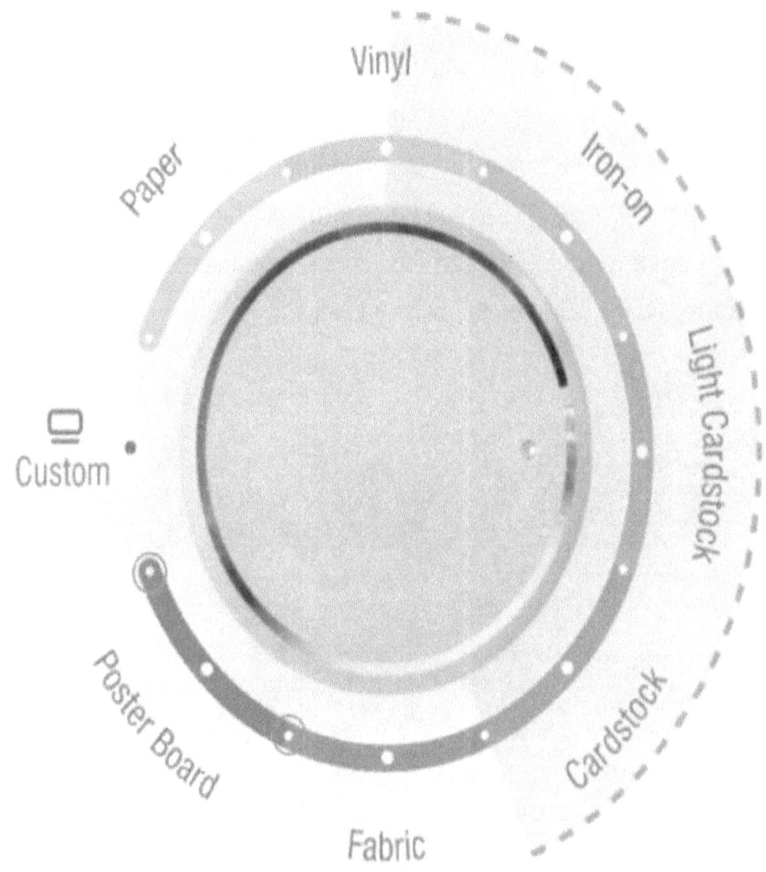

Pressure Dial

Now, let's talk about pressure. Each piece of material will require different pressure settings. If you're not using enough pressure, the blade won't cut into the material, and if you use too much pressure, you'll end up cutting the mat, which isn't what you want to do.

The smart-set dial kind of takes the guesswork out of it. You simply choose the setting that best fits your material, and from there, you let it cut. If you notice you're not getting a deep enough cut, then you'll want to adjust it about half a setting to get a better result. From there, adjust as needed.

But did you know that you can change the pressure on the smart-set dial for custom materials? Let's say you're cutting something that's very different, such as foil, and you want to set the pressure to be incredibly light so that the foil doesn't get shredded. What you do is you load the material in, and you choose the custom setting. You can then choose the material you plan to cut, such as foil – and if it's not on the list, you can add it.

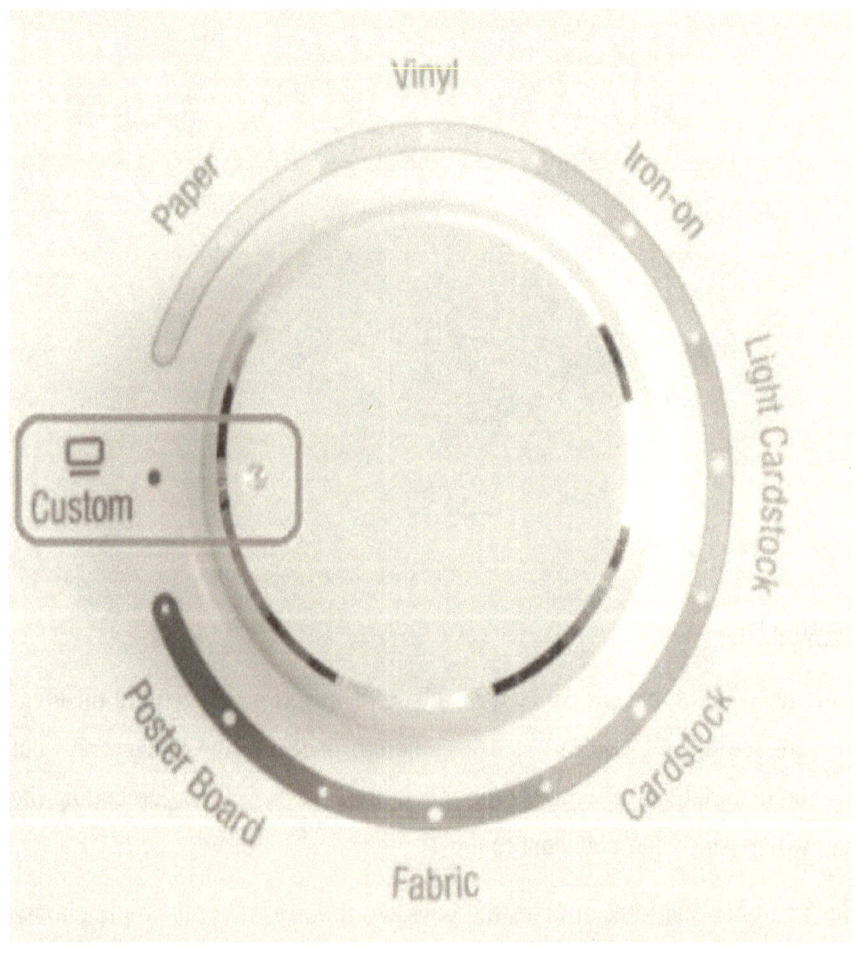

From here, you're given pressure options. Often, people will go too heavy with their custom settings, so I do suggest that you go lighter for the first time and change it as needed. There is a number of draggers that goes from low to high. If you need lots of pressure, obviously let it go higher. If you don't need much pressure, make sure it's left lower. You will also want to adjust the number of times the cut is done on a multi-cut feature item.

This is a way for you to achieve multiple cuts for the item, which can be incredibly helpful for those who are trying to get the right cut, or if the material is incredibly hard to cut. I don't suggest using this for very flimsy and thin material, because it'll just waste your blade and the mat itself.

That's all there is to it! This is a great way to improve on your Cricut designs. Personally, I love to work with custom cuts, and you can always delete these if you feel like they don't work. You just press the change settings button to adjust your pressure, speed, or how many cuts you want, and then choose to save when you're done.

What if you don't like a setting, period? You can delete it, of course!

To delete, go to materials settings, and you'll see a little trash can next to it. Press the trash can, and the setting will be removed.

Adjusting the pressure and cuts is part of why people love using Design Space, and it's a great feature to try.

<u>Cricut Design Space</u>

Design Space lets you do many things with your Cricut machine. Here are a few things you can do with this convenient app:

- Aligning various items right next to one another.

- Attaching items to hold images in place, and lets you use score lines.

- Arranging these to make them sit on the canvas in different layers.

- Canvas, a tool that lets you arrange prints and vectors so you can use the various tools with them.

- Contouring, which is a tool that lets you hide image layers quickly, so they're not cut out.

- Color sync, which lets you use multiple colors in one project to reduce the material differences.

- Cut buttons, which will start cuts.

- Make it button: this is the screen that lets you see the designs being cut.

- Draw lines: lets you draw with the pen to write images and such.

- Fill: lets you fill in a pattern or color on an item.

- Flipping items flip it horizontally or vertically by 180 degrees.

- Group: puts different text and images on a singular layer, and everything is moved at once so that it doesn't affect the layout.

- Linetype: an option that you can do with your piece, whether you want to cut a line, draw a line, or score a line.

- Mirrored image: reverses it, which is very important with transfer vinyl, so everything reads correctly.

- Print then Cut: it's an option that lets you print the design, and from there, the machine cuts it.

- Redo: does an action again and reverses it.

- Reverse Weeding: removes the vinyl that's left behind, and it's used mostly for stencil vinyl

- Score lines: helps you make creases in the papers so you can fold it.

- SVG: this is a scalable vector graphic that lets you cut a file that's scaled to be larger or smaller so that the resolution is kept, and made up of lines that consist of infinite white dots.

- Texts and fonts: let you use put specialized fonts and words within Design Space.

- Weeding: lets you remove the excess vinyl from designs. Press this when you're cutting vinyl.

- Welding: a tool you use when you want to combine two line shapes into one shape, and it's used to make seamless cursive words.

These are most of the functions you can do in Design Space. To use these, simply choose an image or font that you want to use and put it in Design Space. From there, you can do literally whatever you need to do with it – within reason, of course – and then put the image onto the material that you're using. For the purposes of learning, I suggest not getting in too deep with vinyl just yet, and get used to using these tools. You also have pens, which can be implemented to help you write images with a tool that looks sharp and crisp.

<u>Cricut Pens</u>

Pens for your Cricut machine are essentially another way to get creative with your projects. I love to use them for cards, handmade tags for gifts, or even fancy invites and labels.

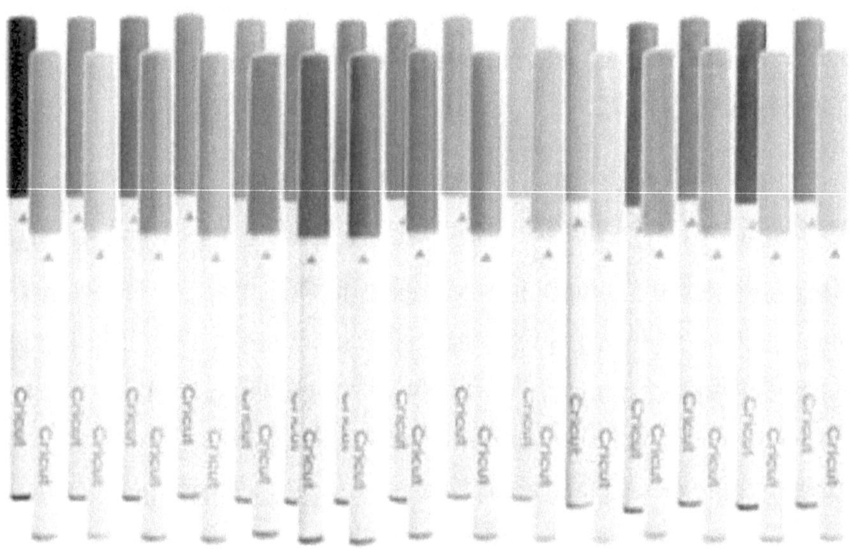

Now, each pen offers a little different finish and point size. They aren't toxic, and they are permanent once they're dried. You've got the extra-fine points for small lettering, up to a medium tip for making thicker lines. There are also glitter and metallic pens, so you have a lot of options to choose from!

But do you have to use them? Well, the answer is no. You can use different pens, but test them on paper first and get adapters to use with them. Cricut pens are your best option.

To use these, choose the wording or design, or whatever you want to do. You want to go to the layers panel that's on the right-hand side, and choose the scissors icon – change that to the write icon. From there, you'll want to choose the pen color that you would like to use.

You can then have the design printed out on the material you're using.

Some people like to use different fonts, whether it be system fonts or Cricut fonts, or the Cricut Access fonts. However, the one thing with Design Space is that it will write what will normally be cut, so you'll get an outline of that font rather than just a solid stroke of writing.

This can add to the design, however – you essentially change the machine from cut to write, and there you go.

You can also use the Cricut writing fonts, which you can choose by going to a blank canvas, and then choosing the text tool on the left-hand side, along with the wording you'd like for this to have.

Once you're in the font edit toolbar, you are given a font selection. You choose the writing font filter, so you have fonts that you can write with. From there, choose the font, and then switch from the scissors to the pen icon, and then select the pen color. That's all there is to it!

You can also use this with Cricut Access – if you're planning on using this a lot, it might be worth it.

To insert the pens into the Cricut machine, you want to choose to make it, and from there, you'll then go to the prepare mat screen. It will say draw instead of writing in the thumbnail this time around, so you press continue in the bottom right-hand corner, then put the pen into clamp A – you just unlock it and then put it in. Wait until it clicks, and that's it!

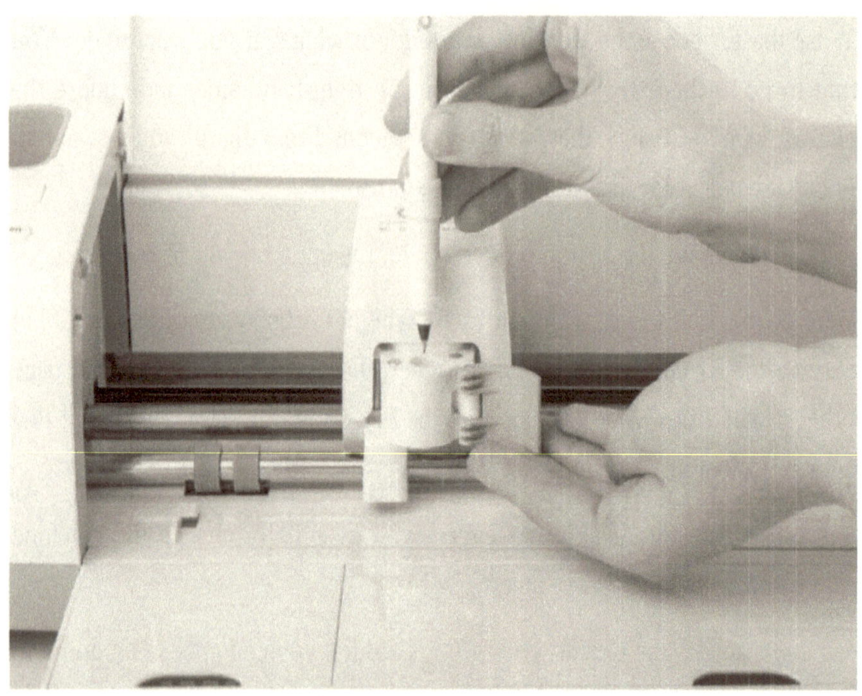

Cricut pens are super easy, and it's a great idea to consider trying these out.

As you can see, there are many different Cricut features and a lot of functions that may seem complex, but as you can see are really not that hard. There are tons of options for your Cricut projects, and a lot that you can get out of this machine.

Layer attributes
Layers
Color Sync
Cut
Write
Score
Print
Group
UnGroup
Duplicate
Delete
See image information
Text - Cricut Sans
Project colors
Pen colors
Black 0.3 Tip
Black 0.4 Tip
Black 0.8 Tip Glitter
Black 1.0 Med. Tip
Black 2.0 Calligraphy
Midnight
Gold 0.8 Tip Glitter
Gold 1.0 Tip
Gold 2.0 Calligraphy
Gold 2.5 Calligraphy
Gold Metallic
Copper Metallic
Moccasin
Tawny 0.4 Tip
Honeysuckle
Yellow
Green
Blue
Red
Blank Canvas
Happy Birthday

Maintenance Of Cricut Machine

Every Cricut machine needs to be cleaned and taken care of in order to keep it working for as long as possible.

Here, you'll learn about the maintenance required for Cricut machines, and what you can do to keep your machine working efficiently.

<u>Cleaning and Care</u>

Cleaning your machine is very important, and you should do it regularly to keep everything in tip-top shape.

If you don't take care of your machine, that's just money down the drain. But what can you do to care for your machine?

Well, I do suggest initially that you make sure to run maintenance on it as much as you can and keep it clean.

There are a few other tips and tricks that can help prolong the machine's life. For starters, keep liquids and food away from the machine – never drink or eat while you use your Cricut machine.

Set up your machine in a location that's free of dust and try to keep it away from excessive coolness or heat, so don't just throw it in the attic or an especially cold basement.

If you're transporting your machine to use it at a different location, never leave it in the car.

Excessive heat will melt the machine's plastic components, so be careful.

Finally, make sure the machine is stored away from sunlight. Keep it out of places in the home where sunlight hits it directly.

For example, if you have an office that is very bright and the sun warms the machine for a long period of time, you'll want to move it so that it doesn't get damaged.

Be gentle with your machine. Remember, it is a machine, so you'll want to make sure that you do take some time and try to keep it nice and in order.

Don't be rough with it, and when working with the machine parts, don't be too rough with them, either.

Caring for your machine isn't just about making sure that the parts don't get dirty, but you should also make sure that you keep everything in good working order.

Cleaning the Machine Itself

In general, the exterior is pretty easy to clean – you just need a damp cloth. Use a soft cloth to wipe it off, and keep in mind that chemical cleaners with benzene, acetone, or carbon tetrachloride should never be used on your Cricut machine.

Any cleaner that is scratchy, as well, should be avoided at all costs. Make sure that you never put any machine components in water.

This should be obvious, but often, people may use a piece of a damp cloth, thinking that it'll be fine when in reality, it isn't.

You should consider getting some non-alcoholic wipes for cleaning your machine.

Always disconnect the power before cleaning, as you would with any machine.

The Cricut machine can then be lightly wiped down. Some people also use a glass cleaner sprayed on a cloth but do be careful to make sure no residue builds up.

If you notice there is some dust there, you can typically get away with a cloth that's soft and clean.

Sometimes, grease can build up – you may notice this on the cartridge bar if you use cartridges a lot.

Use a swab of cotton or a soft cloth to remove it.

<u>Greasing the Machine</u>

If you need to grease your machine, first make sure that it's turned off and the smart carriage is moved to the left.

Use a tissue to wipe this down, and then move it to the right, repeating the process again.

From there, move the carriage to the center and open up a lubrication package.

Put a small amount onto a Q-tip.

Apply a thin coating, greasing everything evenly, and also clean any buildup that may have occurred.

This is usually the issue if you hear grinding noise when cleaning the machine itself.

There are a few other important places that you should make sure to clean, besides the outside and the carriage.

Any places where blades are should be cleaned; you can just move the housing unit of the blade to clean it.

You should also check the drawing area, to make sure there isn't any excessive ink there.

Never use spray cleaner directly on the machine, for obvious reasons.

The bar holding the housing shouldn't be wiped down, but if you do notice an excessive grease, please take the time to make sure that it's cleaned up.

Remember to never touch the gear chain near the back of this unit, either, and never clean with the machine on, for your own safety.

When caring for a Cricut machine, try to do this more frequently if you're using the machine a lot, or twice yearly.

If you notice strange noises coming from the machine, do get a grease packet. You can always contact Cricut and they'll help you figure out the issue, if there is one, with your machine.

Cricut machines are great, but you need to take care in making sure that you keep everything in rightful order.

<u>Cutting Blade</u>

Your blades will tend to dull over time, but this is usually a very slow process.

The best way to prevent it is to have different blades to cut different materials.

Having a different blade for each material is a really good idea. You can get

fine-point ones which are good for smaller items; deep-cut, which is great for leather and other fabrics; bonded fabric, so great for fabric pieces; a rotary blade for those heavy fabrics; and finally, a knife blade, which is good for those really thick items.

In order to maintain your blades, you should clean the housing area for every blade after each use, since they get gunky fast.

Squirting compressed air into the area is a wonderful way to get the dust out of there.

As for the blades, remember foil? Use a little bit of that over the edges of the blade to help clean and polish them up.

To polish them, you should put them on the cutting mat and from there, cut small designs on it.

It actually does help with sharpening them, and it doesn't require you to completely remove them.

You can do this with every single blade, too!

To change the blades in their housings, just open the clamps, pull up, and remove the housing within the machine.

Put a new blade in, and then close it.

That's all it takes. Storing them is also pretty simple.

There is a drop-down doorway at the front area of the machine. It's made for storing the blades within their housings.

Put your loose blades in there first, then utilize the magnet to keep them in place.

The best part about this storage is that your blades are always with the Cricut, even if you take the machine somewhere else.

There is also a blade organizer that you can use, too, made out of chipboard with some holders attached. This is also a wonderful means to store all of your items.

Organizing your Cricut blades is very important, and understanding the best places to keep them is, of course, essential.

Cutting Mat

Your cutting mats need to be cleaned because if you don't clean them frequently, they will attract dirt and lose adhesiveness.

That means you'll have to spend more money on mats, which isn't ideal.

There are different ways to clean them, and we'll go over a few of the different means to clean your mats so you can use them for longer.

Cleaning the Mat Itself

First, if your mat is completely filthy, you need to clean it. Of course, you'll also want to do this for just general maintenance, too. Once it's been cleaned, you'll notice it's sticky again.

Typically, washing it down with either a magic eraser or a kitchen scrubber can do it.

Sometimes, if it's really dirty, you might want to get some rubbing alcohol onto a wipe.

If you notice a chunk of the debris left behind, however, is fabric oriented, hen get some lint rollers or even just stick some scotch tape on there and pull it off.

This can eliminate the issue.

But what about the really tough grime? Well, get some Goo Gone cleaner. Put a little bit on the troublesome spots and wipe it around, and then let the goo stick on there.

From there, get an old card or something to get it off, and then wash the mat.

Once it's dry, check to see if it's sticky. If it is, then great – you don't need to do anything more.

But what if you notice that it's still not sticky? Well, why not restick the cutting mat itself!

Resticking The Mat

To do this, you need to make sure that you tape the edges, so you don't get adhesive near the edges, and mess with the rollers of the machine. Once that's there, use either spray adhesive or glue stick, and then let it dry.

If you notice that it's still not sticky enough when you're finished applying the first coat, apply a second coat.

There are great adhesives out there, such as simple spray adhesive, easy tack, quilt basting, bonding, and also repositionable e glue.

All of these are fairly effective, and if you notice that the mat is actually sticking pretty well, then you're in luck.

However, always make sure that you let this fully dry.

If you don't let the adhesive dry and you start using the mat again, you will run into the problem of the material being stuck to it.

Once it's dried, try it out with some test material.

If you find it too sticky at this point, but either your hands or a shirt on there to help reduce the tackiness.

Caring for Machines and Mats

Here are a couple of other tips to use with your cutting mats.

The first, use different mats. You may notice that you can get more out of one type of mat than another kind, which is something many people don't realize.

Often, if you notice that you get a lot more out of the firmer grip mats, buy more of those.

Finally, halve your mats.

You can save immensely by making sure that they're cut in half. This does work, and it helps pretty well. You can expect anywhere from about 25 to 40 different cuts before you'll need to replace the mat, but cleaning after about half of that can definitely help with improving the quality of your cuts.

The life of the mat, of course, does vary based on the settings and what materials you cut. When you can't get it to stick, try cleaning and resticking it, but if you notice that it's still not doing the job, you're going to need to get a replacement.

Taking care of your Cricut machine will get you more use out of it, so make sure you perform regular maintenance on all your machine's components so it can be used for years.

The Best Cricut Machine To Buy

Purchasing a Cricut Machine may not be very cheap, but choosing your model should mostly depend on your needs, and what you wish to do with these machines. If you have never used a Cricut machine before, then you will need to start with the easiest machine to operate. As a manufacturer of tools and accessories for DIY crafts, Cricut has several models that can serve all kinds of users. From all the Cricut Models, there are four which are most interesting: the ones from the Explore family (Cricut Explore One, Cricut Explore Air, and Cricut Explore Air 2), and of course, the Cricut Maker, which is the best Cricut Machine you can hope for.

Before you even start to think about the price of these models, it would be nice to understand what they can do.

Cricut Explore One

This machine is the most basic one you can get from the Explore family. Derived from its predecessor (Cricut Explore), this tool can be the perfect starter machine for you if you are not familiar with any of the Cricut products. Like most of the Cricut products, it's compatible with Design Space software (and allows you to upload your own images free of charge), can work with Cricut Cartridges, or can cut a pretty wide variety of materials. Plus, it comes with Smart Set Dial, a function you can use to easily configure the settings for each material.

If you just want to start your own small business, and have something pretty interesting in mind but you don't want to invest too much, for now, the Cricut Explore One can be the perfect choice for you. It can be bought for less than $200 on the Cricut website, Amazon, or other retailers. When you have great project ideas, then the sky is the limit when it comes to how much money you can make from your Cricut projects, so spending this amount can be considered a minor and very profitable investment on your part.

Cricut Explore Air

If you are looking for an amazing DIY value, look no further, as the Cricut Explore Air can be the perfect choice for you. In terms of features, this version is a bit more advanced than the original Cricut Explore. It includes the Smart Set Dial, a double tool holder for writing and one-click cutting, and it works with Design Space software (for Mac/iOS/Windows/Android). Obviously, you will be able to upload your own images free of charge, but the machine can also work with Cricut Cartridges and cut plenty of materials. When it comes to connectivity, Cricut Explore Air comes with a Bluetooth option for wireless cutting. This type of connectivity can be very handy in plenty of cases but bear in mind that it might fail if the projects you are trying to create are quite big.

The manufacturer, Amazon, or other retailers can offer great deals on this machine, so don't be shocked if you can find this product at a heavily discounted price. When you think of what it can do, it's definitely worth it to pay a discounted price for Cricut Explore Air.

Cricut Explore Air 2

If you are looking for the best product from the Explore Family, then you will need to try Cricut Explore Air 2. This machine is like an upgraded version of Explore Air, and it's known for its time-saving performance. It has more features than the prior versions, and so far, it's been a very appreciated product by plenty of users. The biggest advantage of this version is that it comes with both Smart Set dial and Fast Mode. So you can easily go through material settings, plus you write and cut 2 times faster, hence its time-saving performance and increased productivity.

Plus, you will get all the existing features of the Explore Family products like:

- Bluetooth connectivity for wireless cutting

- Double tool holding for both writing and one-click cutting

- It allows you to upload your own images using the Design Space software

- It can cut plenty of materials

- It can work with Cricut Cartridges

Therefore, if you are looking for a powerful Cricut Machine that has plenty of features and can be a time-saver, then the Cricut Explore Air 2 is the perfect choice for you. When it comes to the price, this version is a bit more expensive compared to the prior versions, but it totally worth the investment, especially when you buy this product at a discounted price, or with a bundle (this option may include different accessories).

<u>Cricut Maker</u>

Without any doubt, the premium or the flagship machine of Cricut is the Maker. If you are looking to expand your craft business, then this is the right tool for you. The Cricut Maker has plenty of features, as you can see below:

- it has Bluetooth connectivity included, for wireless cutting

- it comes with a double tool holder for writing and one-click cutting

- it allows you to upload your images for free using the Design Space software

- you can cut even more materials compared to the prior versions

- it comes with Fast Mode included, so you can write or cut two times faster

- it has a special Rotary Blade for fabrics

- it includes a Knife Blade for thicker materials

- Simple and Double Scoring Wheel

- Adaptive Tool System, which is a feature for cutting hundreds of other materials

Just FYI, you can use the Fast Mode option from the Cricut Explore Air 2 and Maker to work with cardstock, iron-on, and vinyl.

One of the best things with the Cricut machines is that you can select the color that you like the most, so it's not like you are limited to one color (white or black). Therefore, for the Explore version, you can select between Green and Wild Orchid. The Explore One comes with more color options: Blue, Pink Poppy, Navy Bloom, Coral, or Grey. You will get different color options with Explore Air: Gold, Teal, Wild Orchid, Poppy, and Blue. By far, the Explore Air 2 has the most options you can select from including White Pearl (Martha Stewart), Wisteria, Sunflower, Sky, Rose, Raspberry, Persimmon, Periwinkle, Peacock, Mint, Merlot, Lilac, Gold, Ivory (Anna Griffin), Fuschi, Denim, Coral, Cobalt, Cherry Blossom, Boysenberry, Blue, and Black.

The Cricut Maker only comes with three color options: Rose, Blue, and Champagne. Some colors may be exclusive to specific retailers, so these colors may not be found in the manufacturer's online store.

<u>Choosing the Right Cricut for You</u>

There are several aspects you will need to consider when selecting the right Cricut Machine for you, like:

• your experience with these kinds of machines

• your budget

• what projects you want to create

• what materials you want to cut

When you don't have too much experience with such machines, and you are definitely not familiar with any of the Cricut Machines, then it's wise to choose an entry-level machine from the Explore family. Perhaps this is why they included these machines in the Explore family, as it lets you explore the functions and features of a Cricut Machine. Any of these machines can be considered teasers of the Cricut Maker, which can be easily considered the ultimate cutting machine. If you are a beginner but want to quickly learn and implement some of your great ideas into projects, then the Cricut Explore Air 2 can be considered the perfect option for you. You can easily find a color you prefer, plus you will find all kinds of deals from the Cricut Shop or online retailers, offering you the product at a good price.

However, if you are very familiar with these machines, and you want to cut even thicker materials, then you really need to get the Cricut Maker, especially if you have some projects in mind that can help you make plenty of money. Regardless of the version you select, in most cases the prices are reasonable and you can easily recover your initial investment in such a machine.

Solving The Most Common Problems When Using Cricut

<u>Frequent Cricut Problems and Solutions</u>

Now that you're familiar with Cricut models and the Cricut Design Space, there are some challenges that you might encounter while using your Cricut.

The problems that we will mention will also come with solutions that you can quickly put in place in your home.

<u>Your Transfer Tape isn't working</u>

Using a transfer tape can be complicated and difficult to use sometimes, but the most frustrating part of using it is when it is used on your project, but then, it doesn't come up.

This problem is usually common when working with glitter, vinyl, and even glitter vinyl. When your transfer tape seems not to be working, that's probably because you're using the wrong one.

Some rolls of vinyl, when purchased, come with their transfer tape, or they recommend one for you. But this isn't the same for every case.

For example, when working with some projects, the Standard transfer tape is ideal. This usually happens if you are making use of the standard vinyl.

But, for other types of vinyl, you should probably use the StrongGrip transfer tape made by Cricut.

If you're looking for something cheap and quick, you can use painter's tape or contact paper.

<u>Your Material is Tearing</u>

Different reasons cause this, but the main reason is probably because of your cutting mat. If your cutting mat isn't sticky enough, the material will keep on cutting.

There are many reasons why your mat might not be working right. It could be that you're using the wrong mat for your project or that the mat is old, and the stickiness has already weakened.

The blue Cricut mat is the Light Grip mat. This is good for materials that don't need a lot of stickiness to stay in a place, like paper.

The purple Cricut mat is the Strong Grip mat, which is ideal for those materials that slip around a lot and might get damaged. This includes leather and some types of fabric.

Then there's the green Cricut mat, which is the Standard Grip mat. It's for anything that's not too light and not too strong.

It's essential to use the right mat for your materials, or else, you'll waste a lot of your materials.

There are some other reasons why your materials might be tearing instead of cutting.

<u>The blade</u>

Most often than not, you might have trouble with your blade. When using a blade, two things can go wrong. First, the blade might just be old and in need of replacement. Second, the blade you're using is not suitable for the material that you're cutting.

It's better to use the fine point blade whenever possible, but when you need a heavy hand, you should use the deep cut blade. Try not to use the deep cut blade for a lot of materials, or they will tear.

The settings

If none of the aforementioned works, you should also check the Design Space settings. You might not be using the right cut settings for the material.

Also, if the image that you're trying to cut out is very complicated, the material might cut it wrong because of the settings. So, you should change your cut settings to the cardstock intricate design settings.

The type of material

If nothing else works, then it might be safe to conclude that the material cannot be cut by your Cricut machine. There are over a hundred materials that can work with Cricut, and so this is highly unlikely.

But, if you've exhausted all your options, then you can test your machine with paper. If it cuts appropriately, you will know that the material you're trying to cut is not compatible with Cricut.

Your Blade isn't Cutting Right

If your blade isn't cutting right through the material, then that might cause problems for your design. There are a few solutions to this.

The most common mistake that people make is when they don't push their blade in all the way. If your blade isn't cutting through the material, ensure you placed the blade right.

Also, ensure that your blade is clean. If there is debris around your blade, then your blade won't work correctly. If there is debris, then you can clean the blade using compressed air.

Lastly, it could be your Cricut cut settings. Before cutting, you should check out the settings to make sure that everything is in place. If you want to clarify if the problem is the material, you can test the settings out with a small part of the material that you want to cut.

With these solutions, your blade should work right. If not, then your blade isn't right for the material that you're cutting.

Problems with Images

The images aren't showing on the mat

The first and common problem with images is when they aren't showing on the mat. This happens when you have made a perfect design on Cricut Design Space, but when you cut it, you don't see your images.

If you have this problem, it's straightforward to fix it. Go to your design, click on 'Group,' and then 'Attach' from the layers panel. This will ensure that your designs stay where you placed them, and so when you cut, everything will be where they're supposed to be.

Converting images to SVG

Another problem is one of converting images to an SVG. SVG means Scalable Vector Graphics, and in Cricut, it is a file that is designed mathematically, and it is entirely compatible with Cricut. When you use an SVG file for your images, you will have no problem with the appearance of your pictures.

It's not always easy to find images that are already in SVG format, and so you will have to convert it to SVG using an online tool.

Luckily, many online tools convert PNG and JPG files to SVG, although not all of them work perfectly.

Uploading images on Cricut

There is another problem of how to upload your designs and pictures. This is only possible with a Cricut Access Subscription. With this, you can use images that are not provided for you in Cricut Design Space.

Rest assured because you can always upload your images on your user-friendly Cricut Design Space.

Firstly, make sure that the picture you want to use does not need you to take permission before using it. It's safer to use pictures that you have rights to. When searching Google for images, you have to check out for the photos that you can use without asking for permission.

Also, the files have to be either .jpg, .png, .bmp, or .gif. These images can be edited while the uploading process is going on. If you don't find them, you can use .svg and .dxf files, although they are vectors. This means that as you upload, the layers will be separate.

Next, you open your canvas area to the design you want to add the image to or a blank page. Then you select if you're uploading an image or pattern fill. After that, choose if the image is complex, moderately complex, or simple.

Next, edit the picture so that it can flow with your design. Then, you click on continue; you will then choose if between 'print and cut' or just 'cut.'

If you think you will need your image again, you can save it to the application and use it at any time.

Your Cricut Design Space has stopped working

Every application, including Cricut Design Space, is prone to cashing, freezing or other challenges. There are some reasons why these problems can happen.

<u>Slow internet</u>

This is the most common problem with Cricut Design Space refusing to work. Before you get angry at Cricut, you should check your internet connection.

For the Cricut Design Space to work efficiently, it needs consistent internet speed. This means that both in the area of uploading and downloading, your internet speed must be up to par for your Cricut program to work ideally. If not, you will experience problems like freezing.

If your internet connection is slow, you should place your device close to your modem. If this doesn't work, you should contact your service provider.

The Browser

When using Cricut Design Space, your browser must be up to date to the latest version. You can use any browser when using Cricut. From Chrome and Mozilla to Firefox, any browser works as long as it's up to date.

If you're using a particular browser that is up to date and your Cricut Design Space isn't working, then you should switch to another browser. This usually works.

Your device

The problem can also be on the phone, tablet, or computer that you're using. For Cricut Design Space, there are some specified minimum requirements that your computer must meet.

Apple Computers:

Your Mac computer must meet the following requirements.

- A CPU of 1.83 GHz.

- Free 50MB space.

- Have 4GB RAM.

- Must be Bluetooth capable and have a USB port.

- It must be the Mac OS X 10.12 or something more recent.

<u>Windows Computers:</u>

Your Windows computer must meet the following requirements.

- It must feature an Intel Core series or AMD processor.

- Free 50MB space or more.

- Have 4GB RAM.

- Must be Bluetooth capable and have a USB port.

- It must be Windows 8 or a newer version.

If your system meets these requirements and your Cricut Design Space isn't working still, then it could be because of Background Programs.

You could clear your cache and history, update your system, check for malware, or update your antivirus.

<u>Call Cricut Help Center</u>

If all problems persist, then you call Cricut to fix the problem. The Design Space might be crashing or freezing because of an internal Cricut problem.

FAQ

Is there any software I can use that will allow me to use my own designs? Currently no third party software is compatible with Cricut. This wasn't always the case in the past and has made some unhappy Cricut users.

You can still manipulate designs by welding, kerning, flipping, rotating, grouping and shadowing your images. Visit YouTube and watch the helpful tutorials other crafters have posted to learn even more.

What types of material will a Cricut cut? Your Cricut will cut paper of various thicknesses. It will also cut card stock, vinyl, cardboard and cloth. But for each material you will need to adjust your settings. You may need to use the multi cut function for thicker material. Also, it's a good idea to switch to your deep cut blade for thicker material.

What is a Crop? This is just a get together for Cricut users and scrapbookers to share ideas and have fun.

I'm having trouble using the Craft Room with my Mac? Sadly, you're not alone. Provo Craft has supposedly worked out the issue regarding the security settings. It seems to happen most if Mac users have updated to Maverick on their Mac.

Can I have more than one computer authorized on my Craft Room account? Many people like to have their desktop and their laptop authorized for use in the Craft Room. This shouldn't be a problem since the Craft Room claims they allow two computers for each account. However, many users complain that they have to call customer service and unauthorize a computer every time they switch. This should not be the case; but apparently it is, at least for some users.

What types of projects can you create with a Cricut machine? The sky is the limit. Many people, like me, originally bought it for scrapbooking projects. We wanted to be able to cut out a multitude of shapes and designs.

Why can't I weed my design without it tearing? There are two fairly common causes for this type of issue. Number one is dull blades. The second reason is a build up of residues on your blades.

Is it necessary to turn all my images into SVGs? No, it is not necessary to convert your images to the SVG format if you have a JPG or PNG. However, if it is your wish to have SVG files in your project, there are several free online resources that can help you with this process. Try to keep in mind that if you convert your file type to an SVG, you may have less freedom to manipulate the components of your image.

Where do I go to buy materials? When it comes to buying materials for your Cricut, there are nearly an unlimited number of places where you can get them. Since the Cricut is such a versatile machine with the ability to cut so many materials, you won't be able to go into any crafting or fabric stores without tripping over new materials you can use for your latest and greatest crafts.

As you continue to learn more about how Cricut works and what you can do with it, you will find which materials and brands best suit your needs. From there, you will often find what you need by shopping online to get the best prices and quantities of the materials you prefer, which will help you stretch your dollar as best as you can.

Do I need a printer to use my Cricut? In a word, no. Using your Cricut doesn't require ink from a printer, though there are some materials on the market for Cricut, which are specifically meant to be printed on before using.

If you're not using these items, then you will find that you can get the most out of your machine without that feature.

If you wish to print things, then cut them, this is known as the Print then Cut method and there is a wealth of knowledge about this on the internet. You can make iron-on decals, tattoos, and so much more!

Where can I get images to use with my Cricut? The beautiful thing about the Cricut Design Space and its ability to host so many different file types, is that you can upload images from any source, so long as you have the legal rights to use that image. Pulling images off of Google Image Search is done amongst crafters, but if you're selling the design in any way, you will want to make sure that the images you're using are either open license, or you've purchased them for use and distribution.

Do I have to buy all my fonts through Cricut? Cricut Design Space has an option when looking through your fonts to use fonts that are installed on your computer. This is called "System Fonts." Ant font you can buy, or download can be used through Cricut Design Space with little to no issues. There are many resources for this on the internet as well.

However, if there is a font you're using, do make sure that you have the license to use the font for the purposes you have in mind for that font! Fonts, just like pictures, do have copyrights and can be limited in what they allow you to do with them.

Why is my blade cutting through my backing sheet? This can be due to improper seating on the blade in the housing, so just pop the housing out, re-seat the blade inside, reload, and try again. This can also be due to an improper setting on the material dial. If you're cutting something very thin, but have the dial set to cardstock, your needle could be plunging right through the whole piece of material and its backing!

Why aren't my images showing up right on my mat? It is possible, when you click "Make It," that the print preview of your project doesn't look anything like how you have it laid out in Design Space. If this is the case, go back to Design Space, highlight all your images, click "Group," then click "Attach." This should keep everything right where it needs to be for all your project cutting needs!

I'm just getting started, do I need to buy all of Cricut's accessories right away? No, you won't need all the accessories right at once, and some of them you won't ever need at all, depending on what crafts you intend to do with your Cricut machine. In fact, you can use crafting items you likely already have on hand to get started, buying tools and accessories here and there as you get more use out of your machine! It is, by no means, necessary to spend a small fortune on accessories and tools just to do your first Cricut crafting project!

Can I Use Design Space on My Chromebook? Unfortunately, Cricut's Design Space isn't currently optimized for compatibility with the Chromebook operating system. This is because the need to download the plugin for the application is a current barrier for that operating system, but this isn't to say there is no possibility for compatibility in the near future.

Can I use the Design Space on more than one of my devices? Yes, thanks to Cricut's web-based and cloud-based functionality, all of your designs, elements, fonts, purchases, and images are accessible from any device with an internet connection and your account credentials. This way, it's possible to start a design while you're out and about for the day, then wrap them up when you're back in your crafting space.

How many times can I use an image I buy in the Design Space? Any design asset or element you purchase through the design space is yours to use as many times as you'd like while you have an active account with Cricut Design Space! Feel free to cut as many of every image you'd like!

I accidentally welded two images. How do I unweld them? Unfortunately, there is no dedicated unweld option currently available in Design Space. If you weld an image, however, you can still click "Undo" if you have not saved the changes to your project. It is recommended that you save your images locally at each different stage, so you have clean images to work with for every project.

How do I set design space to operate on the metric system? On your computer (whether it's Windows or Mac), click the three stacked lines in the upper left-hand corner. From there, click "Settings." In those settings, you'll see the option to set inches or centimeters as the default measurement.

If you're using Design Space on your mobile device, you will access your settings from the bottom of your screen. You may need to scroll or swipe to the left to view all your options, but this setting is available on mobile as well!

What types of images can I upload through Cricut's design space iOS or Android apps? Any images that are saved in the Photos or Gallery app on your Apple or Android device can be uploaded! If you have SVG files saved, you can upload those as well.

If you are trying to upload a .PDF or a .TIFF file, it should be noted that Cricut Design Space does not support these.

Can I upload images through the Android app? Yes! Cricut understands how crucial mobile accessibility is to its users, so this feature has been made available on all platforms where you can access Cricut Design Space, including Android!

Select Upload in the bottom list of options, you may need to swipe to find it. Once you've tapped on that, select Open Uploaded Images. Once you're in your uploaded images, find the one you wish to delete. Tap the Info button, which is indicated with a green circle and a lowercase I. From here, you will be able to delete your image with ease!

Are the "despeckle" and "smooth" tools available in Design Space for Windows, Mac and Android? At the time of writing, these features are exclusive to the iOS platform. This means that only Apple devices have this feature, and there is currently no indication as to whether or not this is intended to change in the future.

What is SnapMat? SnapMat is an iOS-exclusive feature that allows you to give yourself a virtual mat preview. This gives you the ability to line up your designs in Design Space, so they'll fit perfectly onto what you have laid on your mat. This feature allows you to place images and text over the snapshot of your mat so you can see exactly how your layout should be in the Design Space.

What Are the Advantages to Using SnapMat? SnapMat gives you certainty in where your images will be placed when you send your design to cut through your Cricut. It will show you where your images will be drawn, cuts will be made, and how text lines up. With SnapMat, you can tell your Cricut to cut out a specific piece of a pattern you have stuck on your mat, write in specific areas of stationery, gift tags, envelopes, or cards, and you can get the absolute most out of your scraps and spare materials that are left from past projects!

Can I include multiple mats at one time with SnapMat? SnapMat can only snap one mat at a time. If you'd like to snap multiple mats, you can do so individually, and work through your designs that way. This ensures that each mat is shot properly and that each one is done with precision.

Can I save the snaps of my mat from the SnapMat feature? SnapMat doesn't currently have a "Save" feature for the images captured in it, so if you would like to retain a photo of your mat, simply take a screenshot in the middle of that process. This will save an image of your mat directly to your photo gallery.

If you find yourself referring to the image for where you have items on your may, it may be advisable to wait until you're ready to cut in order to take your snapshot.

How exact is SnapMat when it comes to where my cut lines will be? The SnapMat technology is quite precise and the lines should be accurate to within a tiny fraction of an inch. If possible, it's best to give yourself as much room as you can to allow for small deviations, but you can trust that the lines are overall very close to where they ought to be.

How can I be sure that SnapMat will work with the Cricut mat I have? SnapMat is compatible with all versions of the Cricut mats that are currently for sale. However, if you have a mat that is a bit older, or which has black gridlines, the app may have a little bit of a harder time differentiating between the grid and your design. It's best to do a couple of test runs with the mat you have, if it's not a Cricut brand mat, to ensure that everything will run smoothly.

What does it mean if SnapMat can't capture my mat? The capture feature of the SnapMat application will automatically capture the picture of your mat, once it's within view and it can detect it. If your app isn't detecting the mat, there could be a few things you need to check. The positioning of the mat is key, so make sure that's done properly, your hand is completely steady, and make sure that there is nothing else in the shot. If you're still having trouble, try these tips:

Add Contrast to Your Mat

If SnapMat can't easily see the difference between the edges of your mat and the surface behind it, you might have difficulty getting the picture to snap. Try laying a darker piece of fabric or material behind the mat so it has a lot of contrast to work with and see if that solves it!

Let There be Light!

If the lighting in your space is too soft or if there isn't enough of it, your camera could be having trouble picking up on the mat that's in front of it. Try adding more light to your crafting space, ideally the light should be placed behind the camera, aimed at the mat. When you're working with intricate projects such as these, having good lighting is best for your eyes, anyway!

Flatten the Mat

If your mat has any curling, or if your mat is unable to lie flat for any reason, the curvature or different in depth could alter the camera's perception of where items are on your mat. If you need to flatten your mat, consider placing it between to very heavy objects to flatten it.

Mind the Edges of Your Grid

The edges of your grid are part of what tell the SnapMat application where the materials are on your mat. So if you have materials that are hanging over the sides of your grid, you might find that your app is having trouble picking up where items are on your mat, or how large your mat actually is.

Look for the Green Square

Once SnapMat detects the edges around your mat, you'll see the green square or rectangle that indicates it's snapping the picture. If you're not seeing that rectangle, the picture has not been captured and further troubleshooting may be needed.

Keep it Level

The blue circles in the SnapMat application are a level. If you use those, ensure that the circles are even and this will tell you if your phone is level and thus, picking up a completely level and true photo of the mat in front of it. This will help you to be sure all the materials on your mat are captured in the right proportions.

My hands shake; how can I use SnapMat?

Don't worry, keeping the camera steady can be a real pain for a lot of users, so we've figured out a way around that. Many crafters have solved this by placing their mat on the floor, just under the edge of their table, while resting the phone or device on the tabletop, with the camera hanging over the edge. In most cases, this keeps your phone so steady that the snap is completed in mere seconds.

What is offline mode for Cricut Design Space? This is a feature that is exclusively available through the iOS platform. With this feature, you can download your items for use in an offline environment later. This is ideal if you're planning on working on your designs in a space that does not have an active internet connection for an extended period of time. In that time, you can still work on your designs without worrying about losing those creative thoughts!